Indian Popular Cinema –
a narrative of cultural change

K. Moti Gokulsing
University of East London, London, UK

and

Wimal Dissanayake
East West Center, University of Hawaii

Trentham Books

First published in 1998 by Trentham Books Limited

Trentham Books Limited
Westview House
734 London Road
Oakhill
Stoke on Trent
Staffordshire
England ST4 5NP

© K. Moti Gokulsing and Wimal Dissanayake 1998

British Cataloguing in Publication Data

A catalogue record for this book is available from the British Library
ISBN 1 85856 096 9

Photograph credits:
Photographs on pages 28, 31, 43, 69, 71, 92, 108, 129, cover and back cover by courtesy of British Film Institute (BFI Stills, Posters and Designs)

Photographs on pages x and 72 by courtesy of Bombay Cine Society

Photograph on page 9 by courtesy of Rinki Roy Bhattacharya

Designed and typeset by Trentham Print Design Ltd., Chester and printed in Great Britain by The Cromwell Press Ltd., Wiltshire

Indian Popular Cinema –
a narrative of cultural change

This book is dedicated to the memory of beloved parents
Kumar and Jankee Gokulsing.

We thank our respective families: Sita, Shishana and Nishani Ramphul
Gokulsing and Doreen, Niru and Sudeera Dissanayake for their patience
and understanding while we were working on this book.

CONTENTS

Acknowledgements

Sources and materials about Indian Cinema are fragmentary and scattered. Consequently, in putting together this general introduction to the Indian Popular Cinema, we have incurred debts of gratitude to a substantial number of people, too many to name individually. The following, however, have helped with both their time and ideas on more than one occassion:

Cary Bazalgette and **Christine James** of the British Film Institute (BFI, London) provided us with the incentive to write this book and gave us some critical feedback in the initial stages. Staff at the BFI Library have also been very helpful.

Dr David Brottman of the University of East London helped by suggesting a framework for the book and providing critical feedback on an earlier draft of the first part of the book.

S. Vidyarthi of Books from India Ltd shared with us his encyclopaedic knowledge of Indian Cinema.

Ravi Vasudevan has made very useful comments and **Professor Sumita Chakravarty** has given advice about sources.

Rinki Roy Bhattacharya has been instrumental in carrying out interviews for us with Jagdeep and Johnny Walker, and acting as a link person for us in Bombay. She has also made comments on some aspects of the draft.

Munni Kabir, whose substantial knowledge of Indian Cinema is a boon to anyone working in this area.

Amit Bose, the former Chief Editor to Bimal Roy, has been particularly helpful in clarifying certain issues.

Iqbal Masud, the noted Indian film critic, has been generous with his feedback.

Cornel DaCosta for his steadfast support.

INDIAN POPULAR CINEMA – A NARRATIVE OF CULTURAL CHANGE

The Centre for South Asian Studies and, in particular, **Professor McGinnety** and **Dr. D. Gosling**, for sponsoring the book.

Wendy Childs of the Department of Education and Community Studies at the University of East London helped with the wordprocessing. **Dr and Mrs D.A. Turner** applied their sound knowledge of computers and design to give the book its shape.

Mr S. Bissoondoyal of the Mauritius Examinations Syndicate was kind enough to underwrite the publication of the book in his capacity as chairman of the Editions de l'Ocean Indien and **Gillian Klein**, the Editorial Director of Trentham Books, has brought a breath of fresh air to the book through her rigorous editorial feedback.

Although the help and support of the people mentioned above are gratefully acknowledged, they are all, according to the publishing tradition, absolved from culpability for any errors or omissions which may remain. We, the named authors, take full responsibility for the book.

from Savitri

Glossary

This glossary is highly selective, but it contains much of the basic terminology used in this book.

Advaita
A school of philosophy which says that God and Man are one, not two

Ahimsa
Non-violence

Alap
Introductory section of a raga

Atma
The individual soul in each being

Atman
Another name for the Brahman, the Universal Spirit

Avatar
Incarnation of God on earth

Backward classes
Members of Scheduled Castes and other low-ranking and disadvantaged groups (sometimes referred to as Other Backward Classes)

Bhagavad Gita
The song of the Lord, containing Lord Krishna's advice to Arjuna on the battlefield

Bhajan
Hindu devotional song

Bhakta
A devotee

Bhakti
Spiritual devotion

Bhangra
Popular music originating in the Punjab, North India

Bharata Natyam
Dance style from South India

Brahma
The Creator in the Hindu Trinity

Brahman
One of four major caste groups. Brahmans are the highest caste group

Crore
A unit of measure equal to 10 million rupees (or 100 Lakh)

Dalit
Sanskrit word meaning *split, broken* but now refers to untouchables (Harijans)

Darshan
Means to see. The act of Darshan has great significance in Hindu religion

Dharma
Has a variety of meanings – may mean religion, duty, law, morality, a divinely ordained code of proper conduct

Devadasi
A girl dedicated to temple, religious establishment or deity to serve for life

Ghazal
Form of Arabic or Persian poetry which has become a popular song form in North India

Guru Granth Sahib
Holy Book of the Sikhs

Indra
A Vedic deity of clouds, rain and thunder

Jati
A kind of social group. Hindu society is comprised of several jatis

Jatra
A very popular traditional drama form of Bengal known for its 'high-pitch dialogue delivery and equally loud and melodramatic acting'

Kali
Dark-complexioned ferocious deity!

Kathak
A classical dance evolved by the traditional story tellers of North India

Kama Sutra
Unique Indian work on the art of love written by Maharshi Vatsyayana in the early centuries of Christian era

Karma
One's actions, duty. It is related to the idea of heaven and hell as well as re-birth

Karma Yoga
The path to God through devotion to duty

Krishna
Epic hero of India

Lakh
A unit of measure equal to 100,000 rupees

Lakshmi
Goddess of beauty, prosperity and wealth

Mantra
Sacred formula addressed to any deity, mystical verse, syllables recited to acquire super national powers, magical formula

Manusmriti
An ancient classical work dealing with law, ethics, morality, customs and so on

Maya
All pervading divine power of illusion which obstructs perception of reality of being

Moksha
Final liberation of the soul

Nautanki
A musical folk drama of North India

Patni
Woman as a wife

Parvati
Consort of Shiva. Also known as Durga, Khali

Puja/Pooja
Offering of flowers, leaves, fruits, music and so on to god

Purana
Ancient books which teach Hinduism to the masses in the form of stories and parables

Raga
A musical scale or a grouping of notes based on certain rules

Samskara
The cycle of birth, death and rebirth

Sanyasi
One who has renounced worldly desires and attachments

Saraswati
Consort of Brahma, Goddess of Learning and Wisdom

Shiva
The great Indian god of destruction

Sitar
North Indian plucked fretted lute-type instrument

Sufi
The mystical sect of Islam

Swadeshi
Literally, of one's own country

Tabla
Pair of drums, North Indian

Tamasha
In Maharashtra, a theatre of entertainment full of dancing, singing and music

Tandava
Classical dance is made up of two constituents – forceful masculine Tandava and graceful feminine Lasya

Thumri
Type of North Indian classical vocal music

Varna
Literally, colour. One of the four large caste groups from which most jatis are believed to derive

Veda
Holy books compiled from divine revelations received by the Rishis or Sages

Vishnu
The Preserver in the Hindu Trinity

Zamindar
Landlord

THE MARVEL OF THE CENTURY.
THE WONDER OF THE WORLD.
LIVING PHOTOGRAPHIC PICTURES
IN
LIFE-SIZED REPRODUCTIONS
BY
Messrs. LUMIERE BROTHERS.

CINEMATOGRAPHE.

A FEW EXHIBITIONS WILL BE GIVEN
AT
WATSON'S HOTEL
TO-NIGHT (7TH instant).
PROGRAMME will be as under:

1. Entry of Cinematographe.
2. Arrival of a Train.
3. The Sea Bath.
4. A Demolition
5. Leaving the Factory.
6. Ladies and Soldiers on Wheels.

The Entertainment will take place at 6, 7, 9,
10 p.m.
ADMISSION ONE RUPEE.

Introduction

Until recently, the study of Indian popular cinema remained largely peripheral to the mainstream of academic concerns. In 1963 Barnouw and Krishnaswamy published their pioneering study Indian Film but the next two decades saw very little work undertaken by scholars, particularly in the West. Since the 1980s, however, there have been some penetrating and illuminating studies of Indian cinema by such film scholars as Binford (1989), Chakravarty (1996), Das Gupta (1991), Dissanayake (1988, 1992, 1993), Nandy (1981, 1987-88, 1997), Rajadhyaksha and Willemen (1994), Rosie Thomas (1985, 1987, 1989), Vasudev (1986, 1995), and Vasudevan (1989, 1991, 1995). In her introduction to the *Quarterly Review of Film and Video* Vol. 11 (1989:1) Mira Reym Binford wrote, 'This special issue is devoted to the Indian Popular Cinema, a national cinema notable for its highly individual development and distinctive forms, which poses a range of interesting questions for the consideration of Western film scholars. It is little known in this country'.

This book, however, is not an academic text. Its main objective is to provide the reader with a general introduction to this little-known but fascinating and highly influential Indian popular cinema, which constitutes the main element of entertainment for at least a sixth of the world's population. Accordingly, it eschews discussion of some of the key concepts of film studies relevant to the textual reading, analysis, interpretation and evolution of Indian films.

Courses in Media and Film Studies have proliferated hugely in schools, colleges and universities in the West. Yet there is still no text on Indian popular cinema, although many courses in Media and Film Studies now allow students to address non-mainstream cinema practice. Accordingly, as well as this overview, so we provide some suggestions for further reading, particularly in Part II.

Indian cinema, like other cinema industries, both reflects and is reflected through the country's political, economic, social and cultural aspects; consequently, helpful information to understanding India as a country is given throughout the book. In Part I, we indicate the importance and relevance of studying Indian popular cinema and offer a general historical development of the Indian cinema, identifying many of its key aspects as well as its distinctiveness in a number of films. In Part II, we address some important themes and concerns pertinent to a critical understanding of Indian popular cinema and explore them in a number of films.

Consequently, given the structure of this book, some themes and issues recur more frequently than others and some films are emphasised more than others. This applies particularly to films which have achieved classical status, like *Mother India* (1957), *Awaara* (The Vagabond, 1951) and *Sholay* (Flame, 1975), but the book covers nine decades of Indian cinema and introduces a number of films which are not frequently discussed but which are clearly landmarks.

One of the problems we have encountered in writing this book is spelling. Given the general lack of standardisation in transliterations of Indian languages into English, as Rajadhyaksha and Willemen (1994) note in their *Encyclopaedia of Indian Cinema*, we have not tried to standardise the spelling of names and films. For example, the forms Awara and Awaara, Sita and Seeta, Parsi and Parsee, Achut Kanya and Achhut Kanya, Agarwala and Agarwalla, Ganguli and Ganguly are used interchangeably. Dates too are sometimes problematic – for example, *Keechaka Vadham* was produced in 1916 according to the *Encyclopaedia of Indian Cinema* (1994) but in 1917 according to Garga (1996). We have provided a glossary to help clarify the Indian terms used. However, for a more comprehensive explanation, the reader is referred to the *Encyclopaedia of Indian Cinema* and to Garga's (1996) equally detailed and extensive study, *So Many Cinemas* for further illuminating information.

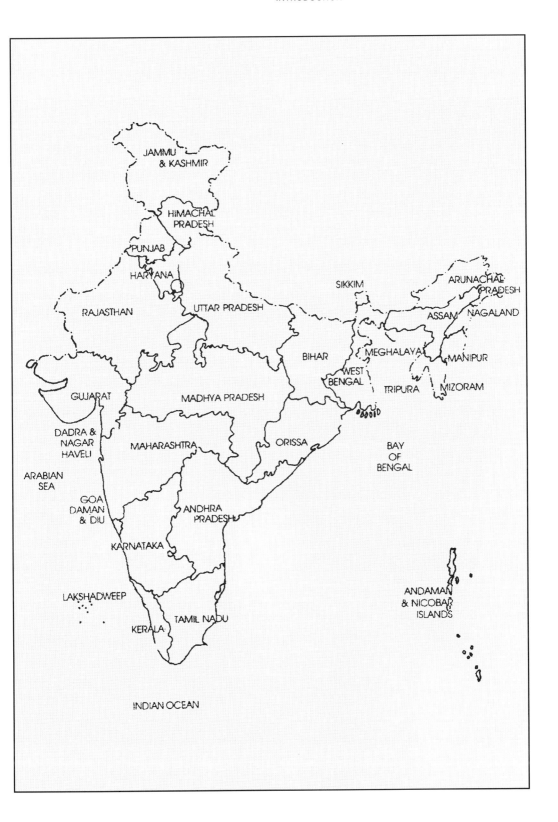

PART I

CHAPTER 1

The Beginnings

A Worthwhile Study

Why should we study Indian Cinema? In what ways does it help us to deepen our knowledge and broaden our understanding of the world? Are there any similarities between Indian cinema and, for example, American cinema in terms of theme, content and style that promote better intercultural exchange? These and similar questions merit our attention. In this preamble we propose to point out the value of studying Indian cinema.

India is the second most populous country in the world and the largest democracy. If present demographic trends hold, India will before long be the most populous country. Perhaps more importantly, India has a rich and diverse cultural tradition that has evolved over 5,000 years. India is pluralist and diverse in a way that few countries are. As Amartya Sen (1993: 39-40) has observed:

> It is not easy to think of another country that has as many flourishing languages and literatures. What is central to our present turmoil is, of course, religious diversity, and there again our position is fairly unique. The vast majority of Indians may be Hindus, but we have more than a hundred million Muslims (India has the third largest Muslim population in the world), we have more Sikhs than any other country, more Jains too, more Parsees as well; India has had Christians for over fifteen hundred years (much longer than Britain has had any) and while the number of Indian Buddhists today may be small, ours is the birthplace of Buddhism. I don't believe there exists another country the religious diversity of which begins to match ours.

People of Indian origins live in Pakistan, Bangladesh, Sri Lanka, Nepal, Malaysia, Singapore, Indonesia, East and South Africa, Mauritius, the Caribbean, as well as in Australia, Europe and North America. Although the vast majority of Indians settled overseas regard their countries of settlement as home, they invariably consider India as their spiritual and cultural home. However, as the recent Encyclopaedia of Indian Cinema (Rajadhyaksha and Willemen, 1994:10) noted, 'For millions of Indians overseas, a major part of India derives from its movies.' These are good reasons why we should study Indian cinema and there is perhaps no better way of studying Indian culture than through its culture-specific cinema.

India is the largest film-producing country in the world; it produces over 900 films annually. Indian films are seen not only in South Asia and South East Asia but also in East Africa, Mauritius, the Caribbean, the Middle East, Britain, Canada, Australia, the United States and the countries associated with the former Soviet Union (see Appendix). Raj Kapoor, one of the most popular actors and directors in the 1950s and 1960s, attained the status of folk-hero in certain parts of the old Soviet Union and elsewhere. Similarly, Dhondy (1985) asks:

> But what of Turkey and the reverence in which the stars of *Awaara* (1951) were held in the bazaars of the Arab world and Africa and in the remote towns and cities of the USSR? This film of the fifties broke box office records (as the phrase goes) in a hundred places, places that ancient Indian colonialism hadn't reached.

Cinema clearly opens a most useful window onto a culture and its study brings us intimacy and immediacy unavailable from most other media of communication. Culture has many definitions: to Raymond Williams, it is a 'whole way of life' and to Clifford Geertz 'the webs of significance that human beings spin around themselves'. By studying a culture we acquire deeper understanding of the customs, behaviour patterns, values, arts and crafts and the practices of everyday life of the people inhabiting that culture.

Take, for example, the caste system invariably associated with India. All societies have systems of social classification whereby people are placed in named social categories with specific attributes. In the case of India, this classificatory function is performed largely by the caste system. Although the caste system is Hindu in origin, it has influenced other religious groups in India as well. Through cinema we can enter the world of the caste system and see how it operates. As early as the 1930s, just two decades after the first Indian film was made, caste became a central issue of cinematic exploration in films like 'The Untouchable Girl' (*Achut Kanya*). A more sophisticated approach to caste can be seen in *Sujata* (of high caste), produced in 1959. Likewise, deeper insights into the complex processes of modernisation, colonialism, nationalism and freedom for women, can be acquired through Indian films. Indeed, the representation of women in Indian films is a fascinating area of study (particularly on a comparative basis with European and American cinema) and has been explored by a number of writers using mainly feminist perspectives. It illuminates dominant forms of patriarchal ideology: how women are seen as subjugated – as either the nurturing mother, the chaste wife, the vamp or the educated modern woman (Rao, 1989).

Cinema not only reflects culture, it also shapes culture. When we consider Indian films, we see how they have promoted modernisation, westernisation, urbanisation, new ways of life, a sense of pan-Indianism, secularisation, the emancipation of women and the rights of minorities and in particular the relationship between Hindus and Muslims. Even in aspects such as fashion and dress, films, aided by such film magazines and fanzines as *Cineblitz, Stardust, Filmfare, Movie*, have played a central role in Indian society and have generated discussions and influenced public opinion on issues like drugs and violence.

How can the study of the Indian cinema enable us to make sense of the relationship between popular cinema and Indian society? Recent advances in Film Studies have drawn our attention to the complexity of the cinematic experience. It is possible to speak of not one India but many Indias. The India portrayed in the classical Indian texts is very different from the India constructed by British travellers, missionaries and administrators and, again, from that described by novelists like E.M. Forster and Paul Scott. Then there is the India cinematised by western filmmakers like David Lean and Richard Attenborough. All these Indias are different from the one represented by filmmakers who are rooted in the soil and who grapple with the day

to day lives of the people. Indian cinema allows us to study India contrastively from a different and distinct angle of vision.

By studying Indian cinema we can enter productively into the thought-worlds and performance-worlds of other traditional arts too. For example, many Indian film directors, from pioneers such as Dadasaheb Phalke to modern directors like Ritwik Ghatak and Kumar Shahani, have sought to deploy creatively the visualisations and the colour symbolisms associated with traditional forms of dance and mime, folk and classical music to enhance the communicated experience. Indian popular cinema has evolved into a distinctively Indian mode of entertainment by imaginatively amalgamating music and dance (see Thomas, 1985) and the works of such directors as Guru Dutt, Raj Kapoor and V. Shantaram bear testimony to this fact. So, through Indian cinema we can enter the larger world of Indian aesthetics.

Likewise, we will broaden our understanding of genres. There are a number of genres and styles of cinema that we constantly encounter in British and American films, such as romantic comedies, gangster films, horror films, westerns, melodramas, film noir, musicals and historical films. While some of these genres are present in Indian cinema, often as a consequence of the impact of western films, Indian filmmakers have created genres and styles that are distinctively their own. This is clearly discernible in the popular tradition of filmmaking in India.

As an art form, film is not indigenous to India in the same way as poetry, drama or dance. It is an importation from the West. However, films quickly became an indigenized art form, appealing to hundreds of thousands of film-goers. Today it is the dominant form of entertainment in India. Of its 900 million people, an average of ten million moviegoers (the population of London) buy tickets every day to watch their favourite stars. Some of the audience 'often pay a whole day's earnings to sit in the dark for nearly three hours' and, in Pendakur's (1989) words,

> are mesmerised by the slick imagery that carries them into another world where men with superhuman qualities successfully conquer all odds, including bad landlords, greedy industrialists, corrupt politicians and sadistic policemen. Women generally are the icing on the cake – upholding traditional virtues of virginity, devotion to God and family and service to men.

However, Indian films are closely associated with modernisation. At the time of partition in 1947, India appeared as the country less likely to sustain democratic institutions. The social cleavages within India, the relationship between Hindus and Muslims, the linguistic differences, were just some of the issues which threatened not only democratic institutions but the state itself. Many writers about the Indian cinema have underlined the important role that Indian films have played in building nationhood. For example, according to Mira Reym Binford (1989), the Hindi film has been seen by some as a great unifier and as a means by which the Indian self, the Indian family, the historically shaped patterns of behaviour including inherited belief systems and scale of values, are adapting to modern society. The ways that a modern Indian consciousness has emerged find ready articulation in Indian films. So anyone interested in understanding the complex phenomenon of modernisation can do no better than examine the experiences narrated in Indian cinema.

So far, our discussion has focused on the importance of Indian cinema for understanding aspects of Indian culture through Indian cinema. Indian films can afford British viewers greater understanding of the different ways in which fundamental issues of life and death are handled. By seeing films from other countries and examining them critically, we may begin to shed the parochialisms and provincialisms associated with our own limited range of experience. By seeing how others in other societies live, we examine our own culture with fresh eyes. A journey into Indian cinema and culture is a journey into ourselves.

Historical Development of Indian Cinema

Indian cinema, like most other cinemas, has evolved over time, responding to various social, cultural and political contexts and challenges. In order to understand the distinctiveness of Indian cinema, its distinguishing traits and privileged concepts, we have to examine the forces that shaped Indian films, and the changes in theme and style over the nine decades of its existence.

Only a few months after the Lumière brothers introduced the art of cinematography in Paris in 1895, cinema made its presence felt in India. The first Indian film show was held on July 7, 1896, and the *Times of India* glowingly referred to it as the 'miracle of the century'. Westerners, who were quick to realise the value of India as a site of filmmaking both because of its natural beauty and its 'exotic' culture, were inspired to make films that used Indian scenery and culture – such as *Coconut Fair* (1897), *Our Indian Empire* (1897), *A Panorama of Indian Scenes and Procession* (1898), and *Poona Races '98'* (1898).

Given the 'magic' quality normally associated with films and the potential mass appeal of cinema, it came as no surprise that Indians soon entered the domain of filmmaking. The first Indian to make a film was Harischandra S.

Bhatvadekhar, popularly known as Save Dada. He was a stills photographer, a dealer in equipment and an exhibitor of films. His interests led him naturally to the art of cinema. His first film, called *The Wrestlers*, was produced in 1899. Next was F.B. Thanawala, who made his debut in 1900. Two of his films, *Splendid New View of Bombay* (1900) and *Taboot Procession* (1900) generated great interest. The first film explored some outstanding landmarks in the city of Bombay, and the second an annual Muslim procession.

In 1901, Hiralal Sen made his mark as a film producer with a deep interest in Indian history and mythology. In 1905 film production was linked with exhibition. J.F. Madan, who had gained a wide reputation in the theatre world of Calcutta, went on to establish the Elphinstone Bioscope Company. In the years that followed, the Madan Theatre began to exercise great influence both inside India and outside. Madan was the first businessman to foresee the imminent business possibilities of filmmaking in India. Not only did he build a vast production empire on the lines of Hollywood but he also imported foreign actresses (Ermline, Patience Cooper and others) 'to act in Indian mythologicals and folk tales, as Indian females were hesitant to expose themselves to the gaze of the film camera' (Vasudev, 1995). For a time, the Elphinstone Company dominated film production in India.

By now, Indian audiences were increasingly being exposed to Western films like *Vendetta, Whirling the Worlds, The Great Train Robbery, Don Juan, Cinderella, Uncle Tom's Cabin*, and *The Sign of the Cross*. The fascination with longer narratives and the desire to see Indian experiences and characters on screen resulted in R.G. Torney's *Pundalik*, shown in 1912 and based on the legend associated with a well-known Maharashtran saint. It was hugely popular among movie-going audiences. Although *Pundalik* was the first feature film to be made by an Indian, it was shot by an Englishman and never shown as an independent film (See Rajadhyaksha and Willemen, 1994:225). The honour of making the first Indian feature film by an Indian goes to Dhundiraj Govind Phalke. His *Raja Harischandra*, released on May 3 1913, was totally Indian in terms of production, and was shown as an independent and self-contained work in its own right.

From his young days, Dhundiraj Govind Phalke was interested in poetry, drama and magic. One day he happened to see a film entitled *Life of Christ* and was inspired to make a film based on the life of Lord Krishna. As he watched *Life of Christ*, images relating to various incidents in Lord Krishna's life flowed into his mind. He came from a Brahmin household, a family of priests with strong religious roots and he brought this, along with his powerful dramatic imagination and his skill in technology, to his project.

His reverie became the 50-minute film *Raja Harischandra* which was instantly successful, due partly to the splendid special effects he created. It laid the foundation for a thriving film industry in India, and for a vastly popular genre of mythological films. One can legitimately say that the mythological film narrating the actions of gods and goddesses is a unique product of Indian cinema in the way that the Western is of Hollywood. Apart from its own characteristic heroes and villains, gods and demons, immediately recognisable costumes and settings, this genre is informed by a powerful moral imagination in which good triumphs over evil, so reinforcing the moral order. This mythological genre still maintains its mass appeal.

The successes of Phalke and Madan served to fortify the foundations of the film industry in India. Mass entertainment and moral edification were amalgamated in a way that assured mass appeal. Once film achieved firm footing as a popular mode of entertainment, filmmakers began to make their presence felt in other parts of the country. In 1917 the first feature film was made in the south: *Keechaka Vadham* was based on the *Mahabharata*. By 1920, that is seven years after the first Indian feature film was produced, Indian cinema appeared to be established on secure foundations – 18 feature films were produced in 1920, 40 films in 1921, and 80 in 1925. As cinema began to grow more and more popular among the masses and a lucrative industry was established, a number of indubitably gifted film directors made their debut; among them Suchat Singh, Dhiren Ganguli, Himansu Rai and V. Shantaram.

A good many films made during this initial period were greatly inspired by the two celebrated epics – the *Ramayana* and the *Mahabharata*. Many of the directors sought to invest their mythological narratives with a clear social message relevant to contemporary society. The filmmakers associated with this phase in the growth of Indian cinema were Janus-faced. They looked back to the past lovingly and sought to reconnect with tradition; at the same time, they sought to draw on the resources and innovations of Hollywood.

Until now all films were silent. In 1931 came the first Indian talkie: *Alam Ara*. It was a costume drama full of fantasy and with many melodious songs to intensify the audience's emotions and it was a stunning success. In that year, 27 films were made in four languages – Hindi, Bengali, Tamil and Telugu. The introduction of sound generated ever increasing emphasis on music and song. The phenomenal success of *Alam Ara* inspired many other directors to follow in its footsteps. Music and fantasy came to be seen as vital elements of the filmic experience. At times, the emphasis on music was overdone. Film historians record that, for example, the film *Indrasabha*

(1932) contained 70 songs. But what is significant is that music came to be regarded as a defining element in Indian cinema. Even to this day, some movie-goers repeatedly go to the same film because of its music.

With the spreading popularity of this new medium of mass entertainment, film directors became more audacious and explored new areas. The 1930s saw the emergence of a fascination with social themes that affected day to day living. V.Shantaram, for example, in his film *Amritmantha* (1934), held up for scrutiny the theological absolutisms and ritualistic excesses that were gathering momentum at the time, while the landmark *Devdas* (1935) sought to explore the self-defeating nature of social conventionalism. The character of Devdas has been reincarnated many times in Indian cinema – 'the dream of surrendering life's troubles to the solace of drink in the arms of a lover/mother is too attractive an escape to banish altogether from our secret lives' (Das Gupta, 1991:29). *Jeevana Nataka* (1942), another significant film of this period, had as its theme the baleful effects of modernisation – a love triangle in which Mohan, driven to alcoholism by his infatuation with the main actress, drives his wife to suicide.

The interplay between tradition and modernity in its various guises began to interest Indian filmmakers more and more, as evident in films like *Maya* (1936) and *Manzil* (1936). At the same time, they were toying with the diverse formulae that would readily appeal to the masses and a film such as *Manmohan* (1936) by Mehboob Khan succeeded in its broad-based appeal largely because Khan was able to fashion a formula. *Manmohan* is an early example of Mehboob Khan's 'women-centred films in which he interrogates aspects of feudal patriarchy' (Rajadhyaksha and Willemen, 1994:250). At the same time Indian filmmakers were paying great attention to stylistic and technical innovation. Their increasing exploitation of the potentiality of the medium and its imaginative reach was to be seen in movies like *Duniya Na Mane* (The Unexpected, 1937) by V. Shantaram and *Jagirdar* (Landlord, 1937) by Mehboob Khan. In *Duniya Na Mane*, for example, V. Shantaram made effective and highly imaginative use of sound, controlling it in much the same way as his visuals. Throughout the film, he used no background music, only atmospheric sounds and voices; even the few songs in the film had no musical accompaniment (Vasudev, 1995:21).

By the 1940s the art of cinematography had clearly established itself as a significant domain of mass entertainment and pleasure. Although cinema as an art form was undoubtedly an importation from the West, it had been indigenised very quickly in order to portray characteristically Indian experiences and sentiments. Even in the very early stages of Indian filmmaking, this was uppermost in the minds of filmmakers. According to D.G. Phalke, conventional accounts of the development of the Indian cinema have tended to emphasize the foreignness of the form to Indian culture – the superimposition of technology and cultural form onto a pre-modern culture. Yet contemporary commercial Indian cinema can arguably be seen as representing a continuity with Indian culture, as Phalke's writings on cinema and culture affirm. He acknowledges the Western origins of cinematic apparatus only to immerse it entirely in Indian culture.

Western influences, however, still loomed large in at least one dimension of the Indian popular cinema in the late 1930s. India's most exciting daredevil from the 1930s to the 1950s was Nadia, daughter of a British father and Greek mother. Billed as fearless Nadia, her story has recently been told by her grand nephew, Rijad Vinci Wadia (1993) in *Fearless: The Hunterwali Story*, a 75 minute film documentary. As one reviewer wrote: 'She was Zorro, Tarzan and John Wayne rolled into one. But her films had a social message too in that they frequently advocated women's emancipation'.

By the 1940s, however, a winning formula for success at the box office had been forged, consisting of song, dance, spectacle, rhetoric and fantasy. A close and significant relationship between the epic consciousness and the art of cinema had been established. Moreover, film was increasingly being recognised as a vital instrument of social criticism. It was against this background that film directors like V.Shantaram, Raj Kapoor, Mehboob Khan, Bimal Roy had chosen to make their films, films that were to generate not only national but also international interest. Raj Kapoor became a celebrity not only in India but also in other parts of South Asia, Southeast Asia, East Africa, the Middle East and the Soviet Union. Gifted film directors such as Bimal Roy, Guru Dutt and Raj Kapoor won increasing recognition for Indian popular cinema in many parts of the world. The foundations of the Indian popular cinema as both entertainment and industry were laid in the 1940s during a period of great social change and trauma for the country. Even as India was moving rapidly towards capitalism and modernisation, it was also coping with issues of nationalism, independence and ethnic and religious divisions. The popular films produced during this period offer an interesting perspective on these changes.

The 1950s

The 1950s are regarded by film historians as the Golden Age of Indian popular cinema. By now cinema was firmly established as art, entertainment and industry. However, cinema is basically an urban art the world over, and during this time urbanisation of Indian consciousness was taking place as never before. This facilitated the development of Indian cinema. Interestingly, some of the most well-known films of the time like *Awaara* (The Vagabond, 1951), *Pyaasa* (Thirst, 1957), *Kaagaz Ke Phool* (Paper Flower, 1959), *Shree 420* (Mr 420 – 420 being the Penal Code for cheats in India – 1955) dealt with city life one way or another. In *Awaara*, for example, the city was both a nightmare and a dream and in *Pyaasa* the unreality of city life is rejected.

While the popular tradition of Indian filmmaking was developing with undiminished vigour, by the mid 1950s, a distinctly 'artistic' cinema took shape, thanks to the pioneering efforts of the Bengali filmmaker Satyajit Ray. His *Pather Panchali* (Song of the Road) of 1955 won for Indian cinema great international recognition and critical acclaim. It was given the 'best human document' award at the 1956 Cannes film festival and went on to win awards at film festivals in San Francisco, Vancouver, Ontario and elsewhere. *Pather Panchali*, based on a well-known Bengali novel, realistically and sensitively chronicles the privations and hardships encountered by a Brahmin family at the beginning of the present century. If Indian popular filmmakers looked towards Hollywood musicals for inspiration, Satyajit Ray's cinematic imagination was stirred by the work of French director Renoir and the Italian neo-realists. *Pather Panchali* along with *Aparajito* (The Unvanquished, 1956) and *Apur Sansar* (The World of Apu, 1959) – generally referred to as the Apu Trilogy – are regarded as masterpieces of world cinema. After making the trilogy, Satyajit Ray went on to create such outstanding works of cinema as *Charulata* (The Lonely Wife, 1964), *Devi* (Goddess, 1960) and *Jalsaghar* (Music Room, 1958). Ray's cinema with its emphasis on realism, psychological probing, visual poetry, outdoor rather than studio shooting, and the use of non-professional actors was in sharp contrast to the practices of Indian popular cinema.

Before his death, Ray was awarded the Lifetime Award by Hollywood and was the only Indian director to be singularly honoured by President Mitterand of France, who flew to Calcutta to bestow on him the Legion of Honour. Satyajit Ray was largely responsible for the creation of an internationally recognised artistic cinema in India. Very quickly, a number of highly talented directors, including Mrinal Sen, Adoor Gopalakrishnan, G. Aravindan, Mani Kaul, Kumar Shahani, Buddhadeb Dasgupta, Gautam

Ghose, Ketan Mehta, Aparna Sen, Govind Nihalani, Shyam Benegal, Vijaya Mehta, Shaji Karun emerged as able expositors of artistic cinema. Their body of work is normally referred to as New Cinema, as characterised by the qualities established by Ray. Another filmmaker and contemporary of Ray, Ritwik Ghatak, has belatedly won national and international recognition for his audacious exploration of political themes, using the strengths of artistic and popular cinema.

It is against this background that we wish to examine in more detail the forces that shaped Indian cinema and gave it its distinctiveness. Accordingly, it is helpful to the understanding of Indian cinema to analyse six forces that have had a profound impact on the growth of Indian cinema. They are:

1. The two celebrated epics – the *Ramayana* and the *Mahabharata*
2. Classical Indian theatre
3. The folk theatre
4. The Parsi theatre of the nineteenth century
5. Hollywood
6. Musical television

1. The Ramayana and the Mahabharata

From the very earliest times, the two epics, the *Ramayana* and the *Mahabharata*, have profoundly influenced the thought, imagination, outlook of the vast mass of Indian people. The two epics are at the heart of classical Indian poetry, drama, art and sculpture, nourishing the imagination of various kinds of artists, and informing the consciousness of the people. They have consequently had a profound impact on the development of Indian cinema and given it a unique Indian identity. Their influence can be usefully analysed at four levels: themes, narrative, ideology and communication. From the very beginning until modern times these epics have continued to provide Indian filmmakers with plots and themes. The very first Indian film, *Raja Harischandra* (1913), was based on the *Ramayana*, and since then scores of filmmakers have mined this and the *Mahabharata* for plots and themes. In addition, certain topics associated with motherhood, patrimony and revenge as, for example, articulated in films such as *Mother India* (1957), *Awaara* (1951) and *Zanjeer* (Chains, 1947) are directly traceable to these epics.

What is distinctive about Indian cinema can be best understood by examining its narrative structure. Despite the fact that, as we discuss later, Indian cinema was greatly influenced by Hollywood, its narrative structures with endless digressions, detours, plots within plots, remain unmistakably Indian. Here again the influence of the *Ramayana* and the *Mahabharata* is very clear. Instead of the linear and direct narratives realistically conceived found in

Hollywood films, Indian popular cinema offers us a structure of narrative which can most productively be understood in terms of the art of story-telling characteristic of the two venerated epics.

Consider next the question of ideology. Despite various attempts at social analysis, highlighting the disparities between the rich and the poor, and underlining the need for social justice, it can legitimately be said that Indian popular cinema is committed to the maintenance of the *status quo*. The nature of the economics of film production and the distribution system being what they are, this is hardly surprising. For example, if we take a film director like Raj Kapoor, who was extremely popular in the 1950s and 1960s, we see how he skilfully deployed melodrama, music and spectacle to create a cinema of security that did not fundamentally challenge the *status quo*. This applies equally to most other filmmakers, past and present, in India. The central ideology underpinning the two epics is one of preserving the existing social order and its privileged values. As Mishra (1985) observes, because the *Ramayana* and the *Mahabharata* were ideological instruments employed for the expansion of values and beliefs endorsed by the ruling classes, there is also a significant way in which the Indian popular cinema legitimises its own existence through a reinscription of its values onto those of the two epics.

The important link that exists between the two epics and mainstream Indian cinema can also be usefully understood in terms of the idea of communication. The epics were transmitted orally and were closely related to ritual and folk performance. Being at the core of Indian culture, they found articulation in a variety of ways and forms in local narratives. What this promoted was the proliferation of diverse narratives and performances within the solidly established matrix of the epics. Similarly, Indian popular cinema can be understood in relation to this analogy between the two epics and their endless performances. The discourse of the Indian popular cinema, as with the epics, has its basic text, and the different movies that are made can be likened to the diverse epic performances and narratives. To discuss the linkages between the two epics and Indian popular cinema in terms of themes, narrative, ideology and communication is to open up an important dimension of the discourse of Indian cinema.

2. Classical Indian Theatre

Sanskrit theatre constitutes one of the richest and most sophisticated expressions of classical Indian culture. It was highly stylised, and its mode of presentation was episodic, laying the utmost emphasis on spectacle. In it, music and mime intermingled to create a distinct theatrical experience. It was highly conventional and specified instructions regarding the portrayal of characters. A number of features of classical Indian drama have an interesting bearing on the structure of Indian popular cinema. Sanskrit plays were highly spectacular dance-dramas as opposed to the tightly-organised realistic plays of the West. As much of the force and vigour of the classical Indian theatre was derived from conventional and traditional vocabulary of theatrical expression, the more one was acquainted with the tradition, the better equipped one was to participate in the dramatic experience. The idea of theatre, the dramatic presentation and the make-believe of Indians were shaped to a large extent by the nature and structure of Sanskrit theatre, and it is not surprising that the classical theatre exercised a formative influence on the sensibility of Indian filmmakers. Some of the traits of classical Indian theatre that we have identified can be seen in Indian cinema as well.

3. Folk Theatre

For a number of reasons, Sanskrit drama began to decline after the tenth century. Concurrently, numerous dramatic forms sprang up or matured in different provinces which, albeit of an unrefined nature, preserved and embodied the essence of the Classical theatrical tradition. The *Yatra* of Bengal, *Ram Lila* and *Krishna Lila* of Uttar Pradesh, *Tamasha* of Maharashtra, *Nautanki* of Rajasthan, *Bhavai* of Gujarat, *Terukkuttu* of Tamilnadu, *Vithinatakam* of Andhra and *Yakshagana* of Karnataka are perhaps the most prominent among them. These regional folk-dramas, which are basically the work of untutored peasants, have one important feature in common: in varying degrees of competence and authenticity, they embody in a living form the characteristic features of the classical Indian theatre. An examination of the central features of these regional folk-dramas brings to light the fact that they have been inflected by, and carry over, the style and techniques of the classical theatre. In the use of song and dance, humour, the structure of narrative, the informing melodramatic imagination, these folk plays had far reaching impact on the sensibility of Indian popular filmmakers.

4. The Parsi Theatre

This came into existence in the nineteenth century. The Parsis were generally rich, talented and versatile, partly because of the lack of a deep-rooted cultural tradition of their own in the Indian soil, and they took up drama in both Hindustani and Gujarati. During the nineteenth century, the Parsis, who had gained a wide reputation as talented playwrights and skilful technicians, influenced the theatre of both north and south India. There were several Parsi theatrical companies touring the country and performing before huge and appreciative audiences. Some of them, like the Elphinstone Dramatic Company of Bombay, visited neighbouring countries and played before large and enthusiastic theatre-going audiences. These dramatists took a practical stance to their work and were primarily motivated by commercial success. The Parsi theatre excelled in historical and social dramas. Stylistically, the plays displayed a curious mixture of realism and fantasy, music and dialogue, narrative and spectacle and stage ingenuity, all combined within the framework of melodrama. The Parsi theatre, with its lilting songs, bawdy humour, bons mots, sensationalism and dazzling stagecraft were designed to appeal to the broad mass of people, and they did. Elitist critics used epithets such as 'hybrid', 'coarse', 'vulgar', 'melodramatic', 'sensational' to describe these plays. The Parsi theatre, which drew upon both Western and Indian forms of entertainment, constituted an effort to appeal to the lowest common denominator. These plays bear a strong resemblance to the generality of Indian films of the popular type. If the folk plays were based in rural areas and presented the vocabulary of traditionally inherited theatrical expression, the Parsi theatre signified an urban theatre exposed to Western modes of entertainment and production of pleasure. Indeed, one of the greatest Indian filmmakers was the Parsi Sohrab Modi, whose *Jhansi Ki Rani* (The Tiger and the Flame, 1953) was India's first technicolour film. A close analysis of the Parsi plays and Indian popular films would bring to light remarkable similarities in terms of themes, narratives, generation of emotion and styles of presentation.

5. Hollywood

Asian audiences were enthralled by the magic of Hollywood cinema. This is certainly the case in India where filmmakers very quickly succeeded in adapting the ethos, resources and inventiveness of Hollywood to suit indigenous tastes, sensibilities and outlooks. Indian filmmakers were fascinated by the technical inventiveness of their Hollywood counterparts and tried to emulate them in creating colourful worlds of fantasy. The glamour associated with the star system and the commercial advantageousness of the studio system were also quickly adopted. On many occasions, story lines, characters and sequences were lifted bodily from Hollywood films and reshaped to suit indigenous sensibilities. In addition, different film directors were enthralled by different aspects and artists associated with Hollywood cinema. For example, Raj Kapoor was a great admirer of the work of Charlie Chaplin, Harold Lloyd, Laurel and Hardy, Buster Keaton and the Marx brothers. It was Chaplin above all who stirred his deepest comic imagination. Raj Kapoor largely succeeded in indigenizing Chaplin in a way that would attract a vast mass of film-goers.

Hollywood musicals held a great fascination for many Indian filmmakers. They related in interesting ways to the defining traits of Indian theatre and performance. The heyday of Hollywood musicals was from the 1930s to 1950s and many had a theme of the world of entertainment itself. The plots of these films were conventional. The music and spectacle enabled the characters in the story, as well as the spectators, to indulge in flights of fancy. The apparent disparity between narrative and spectacle was reconciled through the working out of the plot. This, however, is not a feature commonly seen in Indian films.

While drawing heavily on Hollywood musicals, the Indian popular cinema adopted a different strategy: the plot was not used to heal the split between narrative and spectacle. Instead, song and dance sequences were and are used as natural expressions of emotions and situations emerging from everyday life. The Hollywood musical maintained the facade of reality by legitimating the spectacle, for example *Singing in the Rain* (1952) not only deployed singing and dancing but was actually about singing and dancing. The Indian filmmakers, on the other hand, while seeking to enhance the element of fantasy through music, dance and spectacle, created the impression that songs and dances are the natural and logical mode of articulation of emotion in the given situation. Music constitutes a vital ingredient in the cultural construction of emotion. So although Indian filmmakers drew heavily upon Hollywood musicals, there are points of difference between the two forms of mass entertainment.

Commercial filmmakers in India also departed significantly from some of the conventions and norms adhered to by Hollywood filmmakers. For example, one of the central tenets of Hollywood filmmaking is to conceal the artifice, the constructedness of the effort. All aspects of movie production were regarded as subsidiary to the presentation of a realistic narrative. Consequently, camera angles were largely at eye-level; lighting was unobtrusive; framing focused on the central action of a given scene; cuts were made at logical junctures in the flow of narrative. In this way, the Hollywood filmmakers sought to foster an illusion of reality and to encourage ready identification of audiences with characters on the screen. Indian cinema, on the other hand, grew out of different roots, and there was never a strongly felt need to conform to the 'invisible style' preferred by Hollywood. So while Indian filmmakers were greatly indebted to Hollywood, they also departed in significant ways from the work produced by Hollywood film directors.

6. Musical Television (MTV)

This is a comparatively new force, making its impact felt somewhere in the 1980s. The impact of music television (MTV) disseminated through international channels is very evident in Indian popular films made in the late 1980s and 1990s.

The pace of the films, the quick cutting, dance sequences, camera angles that one associates with modern musical television find clear analogies in modern Indian films. One has only to examine the work of a filmmaker such as Mani Rathnam to recognise this. As modern Indian audiences are more and more exposed to music television programmes and these innovative techniques of presentation, their sensibilities are obviously beginning to be shaped by them. Naturally, contemporary Indian filmmakers, in order to maintain their mass appeal, are drawing significantly on the techniques of MTV. This is hardly surprising since films are where art and technology meet. It is the soundtrack which helps to construct the 'image' of a film and, although the relationship between filmmakers and technology has not always been easy, new technologies – e.g. digital images and virtual reality – are winning. The huge success of *Jurassic Park* in Hindi is recent proof.

Milestones of the Talking Films in India

First talking picture of India	*Alam Ara* (Hindi) directed by Khan Bahadur Ardeshir Irani (1931)
First Bengali Talkie	*Jamai Sasthi* directed by Amar Chaudhuri (1931)
First Tamil Talkie	*Kalidas* directed by H.M.Reddi (1931)
First Telugu Talkie	*Bhaktha Prahlada* directed by H.M. Reddi (1931)
First Marathi Talkie	*Ayodhyecha Raja* directed by V.Shantaram (1932)
First Gujrati Talkie	*Narasinha Mehta* directed by Nanubai Vakil (1932)
First Assamese Talkie	*Joymati* directed by Prasad Agarwala (1935)
First Oriya Talkie	*Sita Bibaha* (1936) directed by Mohan Goswami
First Punjabi Talkie	*Pind Di Kudi* directed by K.D.Mehra (1936)
First Malayalam Talkie	*Balam* directed by Notani (1938)
First Indian Talkie in English	*Karma* directed by J.L. Freer (1933)
First Talkie house in India	Elphinstone Picture Palace, Calcutta
First International Award – Winner Indian Talkie	*Sant Tukaram* adjudged the best Film of the Year in the Fifth International Film Exhibition at Venice 1937

(*Adapted from an Indian list, publication untraceable*)

CHAPTER 2

The Distinctiveness of Indian Popular Cinema

A distinction needs to be drawn between the 'popular' and the 'artistic' traditions of filmmaking in India. Popular films are the films seen and appreciated by the vast mass of Indian movie-goers. They are largely melo-dramatic, often musicals, conveying simple clear moral messages; they represent a distinctly Indian approach to cinema as a form of mass entertainment. The artistic films, which constitute only about ten per cent of the total output, are realistic, often inspired by neo-realism, and seek to capture a segment of Indian reality. These are the kinds of films that are shown at international film festivals in London, Paris, Berlin, Venice, Tokyo and Toronto. Internationally acclaimed filmmakers such as Satyajit Ray, Mrinal Sen, Ritwik Ghatak, Adoor Gopalakrishnan work in the artistic tradition. There are thus very clear differences in terms of theme, style and technique between the two streams of filmmaking in India.

It is in popular cinema that we see most vividly the 'Indianness' of Indian cinema. In terms of the exploration of complex and multifaceted human experiences, depth of psychological motivation and social vision, popular films may be found wanting. However, in terms of popular response and how popular imagination is shaped, they are highly significant. With their unique combination of fantasy, action, song, dance and spectacle, Indian popular films constitute a distinctively Indian form of mass entertainment.

There are a number of genres associated with Indian popular cinema. Most significant are: mythological films with the fantastic narrations of ancient stories; devotional films that foreground the diverse forms of union with divinity; romantic films dealing with erotic passion as they confront social conventions; stunt films where the focus is on the action and physicality;

historical films with fanciful stage settings and costumes, social films that explore important social problems and issues; and family melodramas that seek to explore tensions and upheavals within the matrix of the family. There is nothing specifically Indian about these genres. What is distinctive are the ways in which they have been handled by Indian filmmakers, investing them with a characteristically Indian cultural imprint. Popular films play a central role in the construction of popular Indian consciousness; they are the most dominant and pervasive force responsible for creating in the public mind the notions of heroism, duty, courage, modernity, consumption and glamour. The relationship between Indian popular cinema and modernity is extremely close. Whatever the genre may be, all Indian popular films display a culturally grounded engagement with modernity.

Just as there are a number of significant genres associated with Indian popular cinema, there are a number of significant themes and subjects that find repeated expression. Romantic love, male friendship, motherhood, renunciation, fate, respect for tradition, social injustice are some of the most compelling among them. As with the genres so with the themes – a distinctively culture-specific approach is adopted, giving these Indian films a characteristically Indian outlook. So when examining what is unique about Indian popular cinema we need to pay particular attention to questions of theme and genre.

The Genre of Mythological Films

Mythological films constitute a very important segment of Indian popular cinema. They have their roots in the ancient past in that they deal with characters and events taken from the distant past, very often as inscribed in the epics and scriptures. They depict the actions and interactions of gods, demons and superhuman powers. But they are not merely historical; they portray the interface between the past and the present. The very fact that these traditional stories are presented in a modern and technologised medium like film underlines this. In interesting ways this mythological imagination also informs films based on contemporary experiences. The idea of femininity as represented by Sita and the aspects of alienness and villainy as represented in the image of Ravana are not confined to stories depicting episodes from the *Ramayana* but can also be found in films dealing with modern experiences like *Kartavya* (1985).

The Genre of Devotional Films

One of the best films in this genre is *Sant Tukaram* (1936) directed by V. Damle and S. Fatehlal, which became the first Indian film to win an award at the Venice film festival. It is about a poet-saint who lived in the seventeenth century and who holds the villagers enthralled by his songs of devotion. His wife is somewhat perturbed by his behaviour, and urges him to become more practical and attend to family matters. Tukaram has also to contend with an envious priest and aspiring saint, Salamalo, who hatches various plots against him. Divine intervention results in the saving of Tukaram and the villagers from various catastrophes. As time passes, great leaders come from long distances to sit at the feet of the poet-saint. He is offered wealth and other material blandishments; he rejects them. When the time comes for Saint Tukaram to leave, a divine vehicle is sent for him and he invites his wife to join him. She says she is quite happy with her home and children and she decides to stay on earth. Through a series of intrigues against the low-caste village poet by the high caste temple performer Salamalo, the story is transformed into a memorable film with devotionality at the centre.

The Genre of Social Drama

This genre figured prominently right from the beginning of Indian cinema. What is distinctive about the social dramas is the way that social issues are treated with a characteristically Indian flavour cinematically. *Achut Kanya*, made in 1936, is an early exploration of an important social issue that had been highlighted by leaders such as Gandhi and Nehru. The film deals with the love between a Brahmin boy and an untouchable girl. They cannot unite – caste and religious barriers stand in their way. The Brahmin boy is compelled to marry someone he does not love and the girl is similarly forced into a marriage with someone she dislikes. They happen to meet at a village fair. The girl's husband, insane with jealousy, misconstrues this meeting and attacks his wife's former friend. They fight on a level-crossing. A train comes down the track. The girl tries to separate the two men and is run over and killed. Through this tragedy, the filmmakers call attention to the problem of untouchability. In most of these social dramas with a clear social message, the action unfolds within a framework of melodrama. This is also true of recent films in this genre.

For example, Mani Rathnam's film, *Bombay* (1995) generated a great deal of interest and controversy, both within and outside India. It explores a highly sensitive issue – relations between Hindus and Muslims in India. The film deals with the love between a young Hindu man, a journalist, and a young Muslim woman. Initially, both their families are strongly against their union. They flee to Bombay and get married. They have two children. Later their families are won over to the marriage. Just as things begin to look up for the couple, the fierce and bloody clashes between Hindus and Muslims erupt in the city of Bombay. Director Mani Rathnam has highlighted the self-defeating nature of extremist thinking and xenophobia and stressed the need to take a more rational approach to the whole question of religious loyalties and ethnic affiliations in the context of multiracial, multi-religious India. Once again the story unfolds within the framework of melodrama.

The Erotic/Romantic Genre

Romance and eroticism have always featured strongly in Indian popular cinema. As with most traditions of cinema in the East and the West, romantic films are extremely popular in India and have been so from the very beginning of Indian cinema. Here again, one sees very clearly the shaping hand of culture. Unlike in Western films, overt sexuality is prohibited in Indian films, so much is conveyed through suggestion, innuendo, coded signs and symbols. Songs and dances play a crucial role, eroticism and sexuality often being closely linked with song and dance numbers. In these romantic films, the sentiments expressed and the ways of expression are rooted in traditional culture. Indian film historians observe that in order to understand the true meaning of Indian romantic films we need to reconnect them with tradition. In this regard, the 'Laila-Majnu' and 'Radha-Krishna' traditions are important. In the 'Laila-Majnu' tradition, love is seen as the essential desire of God; earthly love is regarded as a preparation for heavenly love. The absolute devotion of the woman to the man, marital fidelity, loving secretly but without guilt are important aspects of this tradition. The 'Radha-Krishna' tradition, on the other hand, emphasises the here and the now, the desire to capture the joy of each moment as it passes. Love is seen not as tragic but as tender and joyous. In some popular films such as *Barsaat* (Rain, 1949) and *Andaaz* (Imagination, 1949) both traditions are present. This brief discussion of the different genres that go to form popular Indian cinema indicates the importance of reading the cultural inscriptions found in each. It is these cultural inscriptions that give Indian popular cinema its distinctive flavour.

Characterisation

In Indian popular cinema, there are a number of readily identifiable characters who already have specific valuations attached to them. The hero, heroine, villain, comic are commonly found in Indian cinema as well as in most other popular cinema. However, in Indian cinema there are a few characters who are distinctly Indian in outlook both in their conception and in the role they play in propelling the story. The figure of the mother is the most important. She is crucial in the epic, the *Mahabharata* and many classical mythological stories and folk tales. Drawing on these resources also, modern Indian filmmakers have constructed an image of the mother that is highly visible in Indian cinema. She is caring, steadfast in her devotion to the family, nurturing and upholding moral values. A common image is of her praying in the temple or at home and she epitomises the virtues of religiosity and spirituality. At times the mother finds herself in very difficult situations, caught as she is between competing loyalties. For example, in the popular film *Deewar* (The Wall, 1975) the mother is torn between her love for her immoral son and the imperatives of morality and lawfulness. This film deals with the interactions of two brothers – one a smuggler, played by Amitabh Bachchan, and the other a police officer, played by Shashi Kapoor. And the mother is caught in between. In other films, such as *Mother India* (1957), the mother, a hardworking, law-abiding peasant woman, is compelled to shoot her own son when he descends into immorality. We need to pay particular attention to the image of the mother and her distinctiveness, and the kinds of role she plays in the unfolding story (See Thomas, 1989).

Indian popular films are basically morality plays, where good triumphs over evil, and the social order, disrupted by the actions of immoral and villainous people, is restored by the power of goodness. Entertainment and moral edification are combined in a way that has direct appeal to the vast masses of movie-goers and the idea of evil is central in Indian popular filmic discourse. Indian popular films are, as already noted, basically melodramas, and the idea of evil plays a central role in melodramas. As many commentators on melodrama have pointed out, the polarisation between good and bad, the clash between moral and immoral, the antagonism between what is wholesome and what evil is an inescapably dominant ingredient of melodrama. Melodramas by definition deal with characters who are easily recognisable, often stereotypical, and who incarnate the forces of good and evil. Evil is a vital ingredient because melodramas seek to establish the authority of a moral universe. By vanquishing the villain, and the evil he or she embodies, melodramas seek to reassert the moral authority of a world that for a while threatened to fall prey to the dark forces of evil. When we examine Indian popular films this becomes very clear. (For a fuller discussion see Dissanayake, 1993.)

This concept of evil, so central to Indian popular cinema, has been evolving over the years in response to diverse social, cultural and political forces. This is readily illustrated in three of the most well-known popular films: *Kismet* (1943), *Awaara* (1951) and *Sholay* (1975). *Kismet* tells the story of Shekhar, who runs away from home as a child and grows up to be an expert thief. He falls in love with Rani, an ex-dancer who is now almost an invalid, and their relationship fuels the story. *Awaara,* directed by Raj Kapoor and a smash hit

not only in India but in such countries as the former Soviet Union, tells the *Sholay* story of Judge Raghunath, his wife Bharati, the notorious criminal Jagga, the judge's son Raj and his girlfriend Rita. Bharati is abducted by Jagga in revenge for the judge wrongfully convicting him of a crime he did not commit. Jagga later returns the judge's wife but the news of her abduction and pregnancy quickly spreads in the community. Upset by this turn of events, Judge Raghunath decides to discard his wife. In the slums Bharati gives birth to a son, whom she calls Raj. The film depicts the life of Raj and the way it relates to his situation. The third film, *Sholay,* is one of the most popular films ever made in India. *Sholay* can best be described as an Indianised Western, with the visual vocabulary and the attitudes portrayed in such films as *The Wild Bunch* (1969) and *The Magnificent Seven* (1962). The film deals with the lives and conflicts of a group of characters who personify the pervasiveness of evil in society. Thakur Saheb, a retired police officer and rural landlord, hires two trigger-happy jailbirds to hunt down a gang of bandits, led by the much feared Gabbar Singh, who are terrorising villagers. It is interesting to see how in these three films in which the concept of evil is central to the filmic experience, the concept of evil itself has evolved with time and changing circumstances. (For a comprehensive analysis of *Sholay* see Dissanayake and Sahai, 1992.)

Style and Technique

These are as important as the content. Indian popular films are generally melodramatic musicals which are non-naturalistic in the Western sense. The story does not progress in a linear fashion but meanders, with detours and stories within stories. This circular form of narration is commonly found in classical and folk literature. Song, music and dance are significant in conveying the meaning of the story and in generating the desired emotions. Songs fulfil a number of important functions within the filmic experience. They generate emotion; they underline moral messages; they convey eroticism and sexuality whose overt expression is disallowed on the screen; they create the mood for participating in the various episodes. Similarly, dance sequences are important to fulfil a number of different functions. Indian popular films are sometimes referred to contemptuously as 'masalas' (spices). Just as different spices are used in cooking, so the filmmaker, it is contended, uses the standard elements associated with the given formula for success, namely: song, dance, melodrama, stunts, fights, cabaret sequences, exaggerated humour. While there is much substance to this charge, and some of the worst films are nothing but such a formula, the more talented and successful popular filmmakers have deployed these elements with remarkable ingenuity to create a distinctively Indian form of cinema, just as Hong Kong filmmakers have used the styles, techniques and choreography of traditional martial arts to create a distinctively Chinese style of film-making. So when you go to see an Indian popular film, you must do so in the right frame of mind: understand that what you are going to see is not a realistic, western-type film with a linear narrative but a film that conforms to a different set of aesthetic imperatives. (See Thomas, 1985 for a spirited defence of the pleasures and popularity of Indian cinema.)

Until recently, when we talked about Indian popular cinema we meant Hindi films produced in Bombay, and called them 'Bombay Films' or even 'Bollywood'. But this is no longer accurate. A substantial number of popular films are now being produced in the South and in languages such as Tamil and Telugu. Despite the diversity of origin, Indian popular films display readily identifiable characteristics in terms of theme, narrative, style and technique.

Artistic Films

Artistic films differ sharply from popular films. They are realistic, often ethnographic, and they seek to capture important aspects of Indian reality. By and large, they avoid glamour and glitz and use cinema as an artistic medium capable of exploring important areas of Indian experience. They are usually low-budget and are shown at international film festivals. The artistic films, understandably, do not attract the huge audiences that the popular films do. Often they are made in regional languages like Bengali and Malayalam, and do not receive pan-Indian exposure. In terms of the commitment to serious cinema, to making cinema a significant medium of artistic communication, to eschewing the vulgarities and crudities often associated with Indian popular cinema, artistic filmmakers differ significantly from their counter-parts in popular cinema.

Satyajit Ray

When we talk of artistic cinema in India the first name that comes up is Satyajit Ray. This is because he was primarily responsible for fashioning this genre and gaining international recognition for it. His film *Pather Panchali*, made in 1955, was the first such film. In a poll conducted in 1992 by the magazine *Sight and Sound*, *Pather Panchali* was voted one of the ten greatest films of all time. It depicts the childhood world of Apu, the little boy whose life and fortunes are recounted in two subsequent films that together form the Apu trilogy. The second film in the trilogy, *Aparajito*, explores the world of Apu from ten to seventeen years of age, and the third, *Apur Sansar*, narrates his marriage and fatherhood against the backdrop of city life in Calcutta. These films offer a striking contrast to Indian popular films. They use understatement effectively, something totally absent in popular films. There is a visual lyricism and a deep humanism that sophisticated cinema lovers the world over find intensely satisfying. Satyajit Ray made a number of significant films in the same mould that have won for him and Indian cinema great international acclaim. His work provides a sense of the preoccupations of artistic cinema and how they differ from popular cinema. Many of Ray's films are readily available in videocassette.

Satyajit Ray is generally regarded as India's greatest filmmaker and, along with Jean Renoir and Vittorio de Sica, he is rated among the great masters of humanist cinema. His film, *Jalsaghar* (The Music Room, 1958) deals with an arrogant member of the declining aristocracy and portrays both his refined taste and ruinous self-indulgence. *Mahanagar* (The Big City, 1963) explores the impact of urbanisation on consciousness and lifestyles. It concerns Arati, a young girl, who decides to take up a job, much against the wishes of some

Pather Panchali of the elders in the family, thus disrupting the traditional household. His film *Devi* (1960) takes as its theme the problem of religiosity and is set in the 1860s. It is about a happy couple who are living in sheltered comfort but who are tragically engulfed by religious hysteria when the wife is suddenly thought to be a reincarnation of the goddess Kali. *Charulatha* (1964), which many consider to be Ray's most accomplished film, is set in Victorian India and narrates with great sensitivity and cinematic skill the life of a young woman striving to come to terms with her enforced upper class idleness, suppressed artistic propensities, and illicit love for her husband's cousin. *Home and the World* (1984) similarly explores female subjectivity against a political background based on a novel by Rabindranath Tagore. Ray's films, and indeed those of other directors belonging to the artistic tradition, are clearly quite different from popular films.

Other Artistic Filmmakers

A number of highly gifted directors are associated with the artistic cinema. We have already referred to some of them: Ritwik Ghatak, Mrinal Sen, Adoor Gopalakrishnan, Aravindan, Kumar Shahani, Mani Kaul, Buddhaheb Dasgupta, Aparna Sen, Gautam Ghose, Shyam Benegal, Govind Nihalani, Shaji Karun, Vijaya Mehta, Ketan Mehta. All, from their distinctive vantage points, seek to cinematise important areas of Indian reality. Adoor Gopalakrishnan's film, *Rat Trap* (1981), for example, which has won many prestigious awards, is about Unni the pathetic middle-aged man, unmarried, set in his traditional ways, who cannot accept social change and adjust accordingly. He is demanding and authoritarian and is emblematic of the decaying feudal class. The film charts his inability to adapt to social change and the catastrophic consequences. As in Ray's films, we find remarkable use of understatement, a slow meditative camera that weighs the meaning of the most mundane event, avoiding the flashy exuberance normally associated with popular films. Similarly, in his film *Face to Face* (1984), Gopalakrishnan explores the theme of self and modernisation, this time taking a different angle. The film deals with the love and death of Sreedharan, a devoted Communist and loyal party worker, deeply respected by his fellow workers. He leads the trade union at a tile factory but suddenly begins to shun politics. Once again the style of the film follows the neo-realistic tradition.

As we seek to identify the distinguishing features of Indian cinema, we need to keep in mind the main characteristics of its two main branches – the popular and the artistic. Both relate to the Indian reality and consciousness, but in very different ways. The techniques of popular cinema are largely shaped by traditional narrative, whereas those of the artistic cinema are Western in nature, largely neo-realistic. However, in terms of the experiences explored, the artistic films are much closer to Indian reality than the popular films, which are mostly fantasies. Topics such as self and modernisation, alienation, clash of tradition and modernity and the ensuing confusion of values, Westernisation and its impact, the role of the artist in a consumer society, the subjection of women – issues that are central to a deep understanding of contemporary Indian society – find expression in artistic cinema.

In most artistic films, all aspects of movie-production are deemed ancillary to the presentation of realistic narrative. Hence, camera angles are largely at eye-level; lighting unobtrusive; framing concentrated on the main action of a given scene; cuts effected at logical junctures in the flow of action. Popular cinema, which grew out of different roots, never felt a need to follow this pattern of Western filmmaking. The styles of presentation and techniques associated with popular cinema merit our close attention. Indian popular filmmakers, with their inordinate love for dramatic camera movements, extravagant use of colour, flashy editing, and self-conscious use of sound, depart significantly from the 'invisible' style associated with artistic cinema. Indian popular filmmakers aim to create a different kind of film and narrative discourse. The narrative closure, unobtrusive camera, continuity of image, shot centering, frame balance and sequential editing adopted by artistic film directors sought to create in the minds of the spectator the impression that what is being shown on the screen is an objective reporting of real events rather than a created narrative. Indian popular film directors on the other hand do not conceal the fact that what is on the screen is a creation, an invention by the makers of the film.

This chapter has sought to present in broad outline some of the features that give Indian cinema its distinctiveness. For this purpose we categorised Indian cinema into two groups – the popular and the artistic – and discussed the distinguishing features of each in terms of theme, content, and style. The points we have made in this chapter will become clearer still as we exemplify them in a number of films associated with each group. Indian cinema as it has evolved over the past ninety years is a cinema with a distinctive set of characteristics and it reflects an imaginative world very different from that created by British or French or Italian or Japanese cinema. It is a world that bears the Indian cultural inscription.

Unititled advertisment for a film. India Office file no. L P & J 6 1747, pg.418

PART II

CHAPTER 3

Cinema and Society in India

Indian cinema is essentially an institution of modernity. This is because it is at one level 'a machine engaged in the mechanical reproduction of images, and so has an impact on the way traditions of representation are refracted through its mechanisms' (Vasudevan, 1995a).

This chapter is divided into two. In the first part we identify the traditions of representation; these are then explored in some depth in the following chapters. In the second part, we examine the economic and institutional paraphernalia associated with the mechanical reproduction of these representations. The primary purpose of this chapter, refracting the traditions of representation/re-presentation, is to focus on entertainment, since cinema is essentially a spectacle. Consequently, issues dealing with the development of an industry geared to mass produce that spectacle for a market will also be explored. Information and discussion of the economics of film production and the relationship between the government and the film industry are not readily available to the general reader but are valuable to our study.

What are the traditions of representation that Indian cinema refracts? India has a long tradition – five thousand years of history, two hundred years as part of the British Empire and only fifty years as an independent country. Conceptualising Indian society is highly problematic. Labels such as Indian and Asian are loosely used. Furthermore, many writers (for example, Varshney, 1993; Kohli, 1990) believe that these are anxious times for India – the decline of the Congress Party and the problems of governability, the assassination of two previous Prime Ministers, the continuing terrorism in the state of Kashmir, the rise of Hindu fundamentalism and the aggravation of communal violence – yet India has not so far disintegrated as a society. Indeed, it has maintained its national identity and political stability since independence and it is opening up to the world market and is now seen as having much potential for the technological revolution.

Here we focus on those traditions which have a bearing on Indian films and explore how they illuminate the relationship between Indian cinema and Indian society. Two concepts which we regard as central are pluralism and secularism.

The Influence of Religion in Indian Film

India is a religiously plural society – the majority of its people are Hindus. But unlike its 'Christian counterpart where religion is concentrated in churches, religious authority is widely diffused in the Hindu world' (Brown, 1994). Brown notes that the Hindu's religious life is centred on the family and the caste. The church, synagogue or mosque as seats of worship and education have no real Hindu parallel. But who actually is a Hindu? According to Savarkar, father of Hindu nationalism, a Hindu means a person who regards the land from the Indus to the Seas as his fatherland as well as his Holyland.

> This definition is territorial (land between the Indus and the Seas), genealogical (fatherland), and religious (holyland). Hindus, Sikhs, Jains and Buddhists can be part of this definition, for they meet all three criteria (Varshney, 1993).

Other minorities – Parsis, Jews and Christians – are assimilated and have become part of the nation's mainstream. Only the Muslims, according to the Hindu nationalists, are the principal adversary, since they are a substantial minority and they have their homeland in Pakistan.

This line of argument, however, marks a significant departure from the idea of nationhood conceived and propagated since Independence. To Nehru and Gandhi, there were no insiders and outsiders in India; throughout its history India has regularly received and accommodated other religions and in this process:

> Syncretistic forms of culture and syncretistic forms of religious worship have emerged and become part of India. Religious pluralism in India could not only exist, but also if there was a dispute, the state would maintain a posture of equidistance, a principle that came to define India's secularism (Varshney, 1993:235).

The film *Roja* by Mani Rathnam was one of the most popular in the period 1992-3 and it is generally considered to be extraordinarily well made (it was awarded the President's National Integration Award). As the review by

Niranjana (1994) indicates, *Roja* is a text about nationalism, the power of the state and the future of secularism.

The film is set in Kashmir against a backdrop of terrorism. Rishi Kumar, a young scientist, is kidnapped and held captive by terrorists in retaliation for the capture of their leader by Indian security forces. His wife struggles for her husband's release and ultimately succeeds. But what the film does is to point out through the hero the misguided action of the Kashmiri separatists, since Kashmir is part of India. Nevertheless, Mani Rathnam does present the human face of the terrorists and is careful to avoid siding with either the Hindus or the Muslims. *Roja* highlights the centrality of the question of national integration; the story wavers dramatically between the hero's invocations of *Jai Hind* (long live India!) and the cost of being beaten senseless and the bond that developed between the captive and the terrorists.

It is partly in response to the disintegrative tendency of the Kashmir (Muslim) separatists that the Hindutva's commitment to India's territorial integrity can be understood. As Varshney (1993) says 'Most of India is, and has been, Hindu by religion – anywhere between 65 and 70 per cent in the early twentieth century and 82 per cent today'. Consequently, it would be fruitful to state in a summarised form what Hindus believe and then focus on the beliefs and traditions as they are reflected in and refracted through the cinema.

Hinduism

According to Bruce (1995: 84-85) the term 'Hindu' simply means 'of India'. As one would expect, given the size of the Indian subcontinent and the ethnic and linguistic diversity of those who have inhabited it, Hinduism is extraordinarily complex and encompasses almost every possible sort of religious belief and practice, from pagan superstition to ascetic and scholarly traditions.

The heart of the philosophical Hinduism of the Brahmans is *dharma* which, at the cosmic level, means 'self-subsistence', that which has no antecedent cause, and is comparable to the Christian 'Word'. As it says at the start of John's gospel: 'In the beginning was the Word, and the Word was with God and the Word was God'. *Dharma* also means 'universal law' or norm, which applies at the moral, the ritual, and the social levels. Every individual has a *dharma* specific to his/her social status and stage of life. There is also a *dharma* specific to each caste.

As in Buddhism, the individual's spirit (or *Atma*) is thought to be 'really' just an embodiment of the universal soul but, in so far as it has an identity, it is retained through a series of reincarnations.

Underlying reincarnation and everything else is *karma*, which means both action and the consequences of actions. Rebirth is a profoundly moral process in that the accumulation of good *karma* will ensure a better birth next time round. This doctrine is, not surprisingly, favoured by high-caste Brahmans because it explains their privileges as being deserved by their good actions in previous lives and it reconciles the lower orders to their humble position.

The good Hindu life has four ends. In addition to *dharma*, there is *artha* (correct behaviour in the material world of productive and economic activity) and *kama* (the pursuit of love and pleasure). Proper action in these spheres will lead to the fourth end: *moksha* or release from the cycle of rebirth. As in the Buddhist tradition, the culmination of religious activity is final departure from the material world.

There is no single work or canon which contains the authoritative version of divine revelation. Instead of a Pentateuch, Bible or Quran, there are a very large number of sources. The Vedas, the oldest of which date back to 3000 BC, contain hymns, ritual instructions, and philosophical observations. Then there are the two great epics: the *Ramayana* and the *Mahabarata*. The latter tells the story of a great battle in which Prince Arjuna is taught the significance of *dharma* by the God Krishna, who acts as his charioteer. The convoluted story shows the dreadful consequences which result when people follow their own interpretation of duty rather than that laid down by Krishna and teaches that the highest morality lies in doing what has to be done, entirely detached from the consequences.

The Hindu text best known in the West, the *Bhagavad Gita*, is an excerpt from the *Mahabarata* and illustrates the connection between *dharma* and *karma*. Brahmanic Hinduism is complemented by a theistic devotional strand which worships, among many others, Indra (God of Rain), Surya (Sun), Chandra (Moon), Ganesha (the remover of obstacles, depicted as a creature with four arms and an elephant's head), Yama (death), Sarasvati (Goddess of learning and wife of Brahma), and Lakshmi (Goddess of wealth and wife of Vishnu).

The philosophical strand readily encompasses the theistic cults by supposing that the variety of deities are 'really' illusory embodiments of the single spirit of cosmic consciousness. They provide a useful channel for the religious consciousness of the less sophisticated, in the same way that the cult of Mary provides a way to God for the less sophisticated Catholic.

Central to an understanding of Hinduism, as the summary above which we have adapted from Bruce (1995) indicates, is the immense variety of beliefs and practices which form part of the 'Great Tradition', because its roots are in textual religious sources and in the laws of such classical ethical codes as *Manusmriti*. However, the main sources of the Hindu tradition are the two epics, the *Mahabharata* and the *Ramayana* which have informed and influenced Indian cinema since its beginnings. Consequently, we offer a summary of the essential points of these epics.

The **Mahabharata** revolves around the struggles between two princely families, the Pandavas and their cousins, the Kauravas for possession of a kingdom located near the present city of Delhi. The central character of the epic is Lord Krishna, a man of action and a statesman. The climax is the great battle in which Lord Krishna becomes the charioteer of Arjuna, one of the Pandava brothers. The lengthy conversation between them is the subject matter of the *Bhagavad Gita*, which is in many ways the most important aspect of the narrative. For although the Pandavas were victorious, the story of the struggles occupies only about a quarter of the epic, the rest being devoted to Indian philosophical, metaphysical, spiritual and ethical thinking.

The **Ramayana** is shorter than the *Mahabharata* and celebrates the life and exploits of Rama. Prince Rama is exiled by his father for fourteen years at the behest of Rama's step-mother Kaikeji. He leaves with his wife Sita and brother Lakshman. While in the forest, Sita is kidnapped by the demon-king, Ravana of Lanka. Rama, helped by an army of monkeys led by Hanuman, regains her and his kingdom of Ayodhya.

The influence of these two epics in the lives of Indians and on Indian popular cinema cannot be overestimated. The *Mahabharata* embodies the Hindu understanding of the concept of *dharma*. This is what sustains world order. From the *Mahabharata* people learn the rules and the codes of ideal conduct laid down for everybody. It is an encyclopaedia of Indian culture and has been described as the National Epic of India.

Likewise, stories from the *Ramayana* are constantly told and retold and through them people learn the difference between right and wrong, develop a high sense of values and understand what constitutes ideal behaviour. Rama himself is the epitome of all the virtues, an example to all people of honour, courage and loyalty. One of the most important themes in the *Ramayana* is the potential in all human beings for good and evil. The destruction of evil by good, either by oneself or by divine intervention, is a constant theme of Hinduism and of Indian popular cinema.

While much has been written about the influence of the *Mahabharata* and the *Ramayana* on Phalke, father of the Indian film industry – for example his *Lanka Dahan* (The Burning of Lanka, 1917) is taken from a significant episode from the *Ramayana* – recent directors such as Shyam Benegal and Kumar Shahani have also explicitly drawn upon the epics. For example, Benegal's *Kalyug* (Dark Age, 1981) and Shahani's *Tarang* (Wave, 1984)

> use structural and thematic elements from the great Indian epic, the *Mahabharata*, for a modern retelling of the ancient narrative of familial enmity, opposition and self-destruction. The epic provides the framework for a dramatic representation of power and greed in the business world of contemporary India (Chakravarty, 1996:253).

The Relationship Between Cinema and Society

The Role of the Family

We can explore the role of the mother in three films: *Mother India* (1957), *Deewar* (The Walls, 1975) and *Ram Lakhan* (Lord Ram and Lakshman, 1989). In all three, the story revolves around a lone woman bringing up her sons in hostile circumstances. But the ways in which each faces and fights those circumstances demonstrate the changes in Indian society over the past three decades. As observed by Geetha (1990), the picture of Nargis, the mother in *Mother India* is a humanistic one, if politically naive. In *Deewar*, the mother (Nirupa Roy) is less sturdy and withdraws into the world of 'pujas' and prayers – thus becoming marginalised. This theme is further developed in *Ram Lakhan*, where the mother (Rakhee) waits seventeen years for her sons to grow up and avenge her indignities.

The status of the mother and her relationship with her children are interesting. In *Mother India*, the mother does not depend on her husband; in *Deewar* she is defined as a widow towards the end of the film and invested with the traditional signs of Indian widowhood. In *Ram Lakhan*, the mother is already a widow and the 'only justification for her existence after her husband's death seems to be her desire for revenge' (Geetha, 1990:10).

It is fascinating to examine the model of ideal Indian womanhood reflected and refracted through the changing role of both the mother in Indian films and the Indian family in Indian society. The role of the mother is clearly invested with the spiritual qualities of self sacrifice, devotion and religiosity. Right from the earliest Indian films, for example in *Raja Harischandra* (1913), the role of the daughters of India was steadily defined. 'They were to be obedient daughters, self-sacrificing mothers and devoted wives, defined by their relationship to men or to patriarchal social structures' (Geetha, 1990:13).

Mother India   A number of writers (Chatterjee, 1993; Arnold and Hardiman, 1994) have shown how this construction of motherhood and womanhood is central to the colonial discourse on women and how it forms part of the wider processes operating in the world of capitalist social relations beyond Britain and India.

What about the construction of the family itself? Illumination can be found in the 1994 film *Hum Aapke Hain Koun* (HAHK – who am I to you?) which achieved considerable commercial success and has been compared to such blockbusters as *Sholay* (1975) and *Mughal-e-Azam* (1960). At the seminar on Popular Culture in India at the School for Oriental and African Studies (SOAS) in June 1995, Uberoi presented an illuminating paper on the film *HAHK* and we draw upon this here.

There are a number of surprising elements about *HAHK*. It is a modest budget family drama without the 'masala' ingredients of sex, sadism and violence so characteristic of recent 'Bollywood' films. It has a considerable number of melodious songs and catchy tunes, but no more than *Roja* (1992) or *1942: A Love Story* (1994). What is most surprising is that it is a 'clean family movie'. In describing the film as clean and morally uplifting, Uberoi has drawn attention to a number of themes in the film, including the following:

a) **The family as tradition**. There is consensus among viewers that HAHK is about not only joint family but also Indian culture and tradition. The possible break-up of the Indian joint family system due to processes of urbanisation, industrialisation and westernisation has been causing concern for the past fifty years. However, the film is more about what the family should be rather than what it is; hence, there is no antagonism between the father figure and the sons, for example, no tension between the brothers and no tension between mother-in-law and daughter-in-law. Perhaps the best comment comes from Madhuri Dixit, who won the filmfare award for Best Actress of 1994: 'Hum Aapke Hain Koun presents a perfect 'utopia' – about simple values and guileless people'.

b) **Vulgarity.** Sex and vulgarity have been part and parcel of all popular cinema since it began. Indian cinema has had its fair share, but in recent years the Indian public has witnessed more of it through satellite and cable TV channels. Uberoi claims that an important aspect of *HAHK* as a 'family' film is that the whole family (grandparents, parents and children) can watch it together without embarrassment. Despite its highly simplified structure, the film is a universal love story but, as Uberoi rightly suggests, 'the conflicts in the film are those between *dharma* (duty) and desire and between freedom and destiny – conflicts which have to be reconciled before a love story can come to a satisfactory happy ending'.

But perhaps the most important aspect of *HAHK* is how it reinforces India's cultural heritage through depicting series of rituals – betrothal, engagement, the *mehndi* (the decoration of the bride's hands with leaves of the Henna), marriage ceremonies and the celebration of the new-born child. Indeed, according to Uberoi, 'the most remarkable instance is the marriage ceremony itself, the centre-piece and indeed the *raison d'être* of the movie'.

Hindi films are seen as 'collective fantasies' since they have many features in common with fairy tales. Like fairy tales, Hindi films have the psychological function of producing a sense of security by upholding the picture of a world in which the family and *dharma* are safe (Kakar mentioned in Valicha, 1988:35) and that there are parallels between the Hindi film and certain popular myths.

The Role of Language in Hindi Films

How do films communicate the collective fantasies which, according to Kakar, characterise Indian popular cinema? Language has a significant bearing on the relationship between cinema and society in India. Adequate and appropriate communication is possible only through the languages of the people, their mother tongues and, as Oomen (1990:131-132) rightly notes, the polyglot character of the Indian nation-state renders the challenge particularly stupendous: 'we are here referring to 800 million people, one-sixth of humanity'.

A conservative estimate puts the number of languages in India at over 100. However, the Indian constitution recognises only 15 major languages, with Hindi spoken by about 40 per cent of the population. Consequently, although the South of India is more prolific in terms of film production – in Tamil, Telugu, Malayalam and Kannada – and, although Calcutta is normally seen to lead the rest of India as a centre for quality, the grip of Bombay with its emphasis on Hindi is tighter. In 1993, films in Hindi numbered only 182 out of over 800 but they cater to 'the all-Indian market and are understood by the majority of the Indian population (an achievement in India's polylingual society for which the Bombay film itself has claimed its fair share of credit)' (Chakravarty, 1996:9).

The subject and treatment of popular Hindi films are tried, trusted and predictable – a planned mixture of stars, songs, dances and titillation – the story is just a peg on which to hang these elements. The stars themselves (and their ratings) are the most important aspect of any film – they are sought after and relentlessly pursued: Amitabh Bachchan, Sanjay Dutt, Salman Khan, Sharukh Khan, Madhuri Dixit.

Until the 1970s, love stories were very popular and in India, where arranged marriages are still common, Indian films have created a new legitimacy for love-marriage through various devices. According to Nandy (1981), the best-known devices include the following:

a) the couple discover that their parents had planned to get them married to each other anyway.

b) the hero, separated from the heroine by barriers of caste, status or wealth, does a good turn to the girl's family, so that the family, in the last scene, guiltily give their girl in marriage to him as a reward

c) alternatively, it is the heroine who does a good turn to win the hearts of the hero's arrogant family.

Another strategy of Indian narrative structure is the double roles, particularly with regard to the main male protagonists – often two sons, one good and the other bad, one meek and the other aggressive. Sometimes it is the 'lost-'n'-found', 'cops and robbers' formulae with crime being the fulcrum for all kinds of plots.

Scenes of Violence

Many critics have commented on the gratuitous scenes of violence and gory deaths which have characterised the Indian popular cinema since the 1970s. This period saw the rise of Amitabh Bachchan as the 'angry young man' who went on to become the last of the superstars and, according to the Indian press, 'a colossus who may not be seen again'. It marked a decisive break with the past. Any love triangle occupies a secondary position; in many of the films of the 1970s and early 1980s, hero Bachchan has little time for speeches. Using his height and his voice to full advantage, he concentrated on what the plot required him to do – generally to settle a score or redress an injustice. Violence reached its apogee in *Sholay* (Flames, 1975) a film which has become a legend. Bachchan was no longer the avenger seeking justice but a mercenary, selling his prowess as a killer, for a price (Garga, 1996:184). One of the most noticeable features of *Sholay* is that while the two heroes (Bachchan and Dharmendra) still value friendship and male bonding (*dosti*), there is no regard for family values (see Dissanayake and Sahai, 1992 for a cultural reading of *Sholay*).

We said at the beginning of this chapter that the cinema refracts the traditions of representation. One reason for the enormous success of these Amitabh Bachchan films is that the 1970s were a period of deep crisis in India. There was urban crime, spiralling inflation, corrupt and sectarian politics – to such an extent that Mrs Gandhi, then Prime Minister, imposed a State of Emergency in 1975. Out of the window went the kind of romanticism associated with Rajesh Khanna, for example. The public was looking for a hero to put things right and Amitabh Bachchan fitted the bill perfectly.

But Amitabh Bachchan's films did not eliminate the significance of music and dance. According to Barnouw and Krishnaswamy (1963), music is an integral element of Indian film – its importance is due to the structure of Indian traditional performance. Indeed, 'classical Sanskrit theatre made no separation between the arts of music, song and dance – all were required for a perfect enactment of the performance themes, whether they were sacred or secular in nature' (Beeman, 1981). We devote a sub-section to the importance of the role of music, song and dance in Indian cinema later in this book. Here, it is sufficient to identify some of the aspects of music, song and dance in Indian cinema.

In a paper for a Postgraduate Seminar at the Institute of Commonwealth Studies in 1991, Kabir outlined the development of Indian Film music from its early days until 1991. She drew attention to how, ever since the introduction of sound in *Alam Ara* (1931), films became dependent 'on the song in a way that has differentiated Indian cinema from most world cinema'. Remember that *Indrasabha* (The Court of Lord Indra) produced in 1932 had 70 songs!

How the songs were sung changed. In the early thirties and forties, the songs were recorded live during the filming of the song sequence and the 'song would be picturised in a single take, which meant that the song sequence would be virtually static' (Kabir, 1991:1). Since the 1950s, playback singing has become an established feature of music production and this has produced a host of playback singers, including Mukesh, Rafi, Lata Mangeshkar, Kishore Kumar, Kumar Shanu, Udit Narayan, Kavita Krishnamurthy and Alka Yagnik, many of whom have achieved international reputation in their own right.

Dance is equally important in Indian films. Sanskrit theatre integrated dance music and acting – *Natya* and *Sangeet* – separation only recently has occurred. Dance is an inseparable aspect of Indian culture and is manifested in all Indian festivals and religious occasions. Classical dancing was originally associated with the Devdasis in the south and with the Kothivalis in the north. Many men dancers were eunuchs and the dancing women could not lead normal lives. The dance of the eunuchs and of the Kothivalis was called *Nautch*.

Through a mixture of dance forms from the West and other parts of the world, the Indian film industry has popularised and liberated Indian dance from its low status. In 1948, the costliest and most spectacular film of the period, *Chandralekha*, dramatically changed the nature of film production. Nearly three and a half hours long, the film culminated in a spectacular dance which later film producers tried to emulate but never equalled.

The Economics of the Film Industry and the State

Filmmaking is very costly. In the beginning, Indian films were financed from sources connected with the film industry, both the distribution and exhibition sectors contributing to the making of films. By the time of the Second World War, the film industry had, in the words of Majumdar (1995:301), 'a look of solidarity and self respect and among the Indian industries, cinema occupied the 8th place reckoned in terms of investment in the early forties'.

However, the Indian film business has never been officially considered an industry, so raising money from financial institutions has always been problematic. This, coupled with the high rate of failures at the box office, particularly in recent years, has made the financing of films very risky.

The Second World War created a boom in the film industry which, because it had no standardised practices, provided fertile ground for people with 'hot money'. This led, according to Majumdar (1995), to the decline of the studio system, where actors and crew were employees, and the rise of the star system, with stars becoming freelance artists who performed in more than one film at a time. Consequently, the star, the music director and the playback singer became the beneficiaries of the new order (p.302).

Meanwhile, the import of foreign films was, until 1957, allowed freely through Indian importers as well as some foreign companies. In 1960, the government established the Film Finance Corporation (FFC) and in the middle of the 1960s, an informal system of canalisation of films through the State Trading Corporation was introduced; subsequently, the National Film Development Corporation (NFDC) replaced the FFC and canalised the import of feature films, but this ceased in 1992.

The government's casual approach to the film industry is evident from the fact (reported by Majumdar, 1995) that there are no reliable data on such basic information as the total capital invested in the film industry in India, the annual investment in filmmaking gross collections or the sources from which production is obtained. Very little research has been carried out in this rather nebulous but extremely important area. *The Economics of Film Industry in India* (Jain, 1960) provided an overview of the field. Jain examined matters such as the technology of filmmaking, the raw materials and equipment required, as well as wages and welfare issues. He also provided useful information on the average costs of films, marketing and taxation and some international comparisons. Though limited in scope – it provided very little information on the exhibitions and their interrelationship with the producers and distributors – the book is a landmark.

Dharap's *Indian Films* provides extensive statistical information on various aspects of the film industry such as the number of cinema halls, the number of films produced in India and estimated costs of film production. First published in 1973, subsequent volumes (1974, 1975, 1977, 1979 and 1985) are 'only statistical updates'. In *Economics of Indian Cinema*, Oomen and Joseph (1991) deal with Malayalam films only, but in their introduction and in chapter two they give a useful overview of the commercialisation of the film industry in India. Recently, however, Mital's (1995) *Cinema Industry in India* focuses primarily on pricing and taxation, and he too notes that the 'economics of entertainment is a highly under-researched area of study' and that literature on this subject is 'scant and academic works are few and far between.'

Maitra's (1995) *100 years of Cinema* offers a useful summary of the cinema-going public and India's cinemas. He asserts that India has a cinema-going population of 65 million per week, though the cinemas number about 13,000 of which 6,500 are permanent and the rest touring. This works out to seven seats per thousand of the population, a very low rate compared to other large countries and considering that they are spread over 22 states and nine union territories. Half of the theatres are in the South.

Film budgets range between 3 crores (Rs30,000,000 i.e. about £540,000) and 6 lakhs (Rs600,000 i.e. about £11,000), the multi-star spectacle 'standing at one extreme end – the shoestring art and realism saga at the other!'. A moderately successful film earns much more than its costs and various outlets which have recently opened up have created new avenues for revenue, like the video market at home and overseas, audio rights, telecast on Doordashan (the National Television system) and various satellite TV channels.

So why do people go to the movies? Until the arrival of television, cinema-going was a regular and habit-forming part of people's lives all over the world. The excitement, the novelty and the entertainment which the technology of film production provided had no parallel in people's lives. For the young, cinema halls were places of romance where young people could get together secretly, sheltered by the relative anonymity of the crowd and the dark environment. There were (and still are) films which catered for the gratification of urban youth culture.

Cinema-going was (and to some extent still is) also part of family entertainment. The impact of these social occasions on the lives of people is under researched, but it is clear from a number of interviews carried out, particularly for television programmes – for example the one by Munni Kabir for her programme Movie Mahal on Channel 4 – that many people remember their childhood visits to the cinema in the company of their parents. As they grew up, many saw films which, according to their parents and the Board of Censors, they should not have seen. Consequently, at some stage in the lives of the vast majority of people, cinema-going was almost an act of transgression against parental authority.

The Movie Moguls

Who are these moguls who built cinema halls and financed the industry? The situation in India is different from that in the West. With the arrival of television in the West in the 1950s and 1960s, cinema attendance dropped and many cinemas closed down. However, in recent years, the film industry has fought back with blockbusters such as *Jurassic Park*. In India, however, television is not yet widespread; consequently, cinema attendance has so far not suffered materially. It is true that satellite, cable and video facilities are having an impact on the cinema-going public, but they seem to have made this public more discriminating. Cinema-going is still far more important to people than television.

The earlier movie moguls operated in the studio system. Garga (1996) documents the activities of some of the better known – J. F. Madhan of the Elphinstone Company, Chandulal Shah of Ranjit Movietone, B. N. Sircar, Devaki Bose, P.C. Barua, Nitin Bose of New Theatres, Damle, Fatehlal and Shantaram of Prabhat Studio and Himansu Rai of Bombay Talkies. But there is little reliable information on the financial entrepreneurs of recent decades. Das Gupta (1991:268) asserts that 'the finance for these films comes largely from a parallel economy lying outside the pale of the legitimate organised sector of banking and insurance and manufacturing industries'. Recent reports by the press are disturbing. Producer Mukesh Duggal was gunned down at Andheri, allegedly for refusing to give extortion money. The Dawood Ibrahim gang is reported to be increasingly targeting Hindi film producers and financiers for extortion money and the situation has deteriorated to such an extent that certain producers have fled abroad. According to the *Financial Times* of 13 August (1997: 6), Gulshan Kumar, India's 'Cassette King' and a movie mogul was shot dead, reportedly by Bombay gangsters. *The Financial Times* comments that 'Bombay's thriving movie industry has long had connections with organised crime, largely through the laundering of 'black' money used to finance many of the all-singing, all-dancing Hindi musicals which make Bollywood the world's most prolific film capital'.

Film Censorship

If the operations of the movie moguls are not always transparent, those of the government with regard to film censorship are quite clear. During colonial times, the British rulers were determined that cinema should serve their colonial policy. In the early years of Indian cinema, vigorous attempts were made by the rulers to regulate cinema for a variety of reasons, chief among them the desire to preserve the 'prestige of the white woman'. Constance

Bromley, former secretary and manager of the Opera House in Calcutta, a premier picture house, wrote an inflammatory newspaper article upon her return to England headlined: 'Films That Lower Our Prestige in India: Imperilling the Prestige of the White Woman' (quoted by Arora, 1995).

As the influence of the British began to decline in India, cinema was credited with spreading communism. According to the author of a classified report *The Cinema in the East: Factors in the Spread of Communism* (quoted by Arora, 1995)

> ...there can be no doubt that the way for Communist influence has been greatly facilitated by a powerful and novel element, which in recent years has entered into the lives of semi-civilized people in all parts of the tropical world. That element is the cinema.

Arora (1995:47) comments perceptively:

It is chronic that whereas the native was believed incapable of comprehending such genres of American cinema as romantic comedy or social parody, s/he was nevertheless credited with comprehending the narrative of such Soviet films as *Battleship Potemkin* and *Ivan the Terrible* and consequently being swayed by 'Communist propaganda'.

All these factors help to explain why, half a century after the departure of the British, Indian cinema is still one of the most heavily censored. The Film Censor Board of India continues 'to impose restrictions on the depiction of adult sexuality in a weak, though desperate, attempt at maintaining an essentialist and nationalistic distinction between western and Indian character types' (Arora, 1995:48). The Indian film industry subverts this control mainly through its song and dance sequences.

CHAPTER 4

Religion, Ethnicity and Caste in Indian Cinema

India is a multi-ethnic, multi-lingual and multi-religious society. Questions of religion, language and ethnicity play a significant part in the lives of the people, often generating tensions and acrimony. In addition, there is the question of caste, a distinguishing feature of the Hindu social order. As issues of caste, ethnicity and religion meet contemporary modernising forces, a sense of confrontation naturally emerges. These vital social issues find expression in Indian cinema. As we have argued, cinema both reflects and shapes society and Indian films have mirrored the religious, ethnic and caste tensions in society and also intervened in debates related to them, so shaping the discussion. This chapter looks at religious divisions, ethnic and caste conflicts and how enlightened film directors in India are seeking to create a better understanding of these issues.

The rather elusive nature of the concepts of religion, ethnicity and caste adds to the complexity. Accordingly, we try to clarify the terms and some relevant details so that their pertinence to Indian cinema can be understood.

Religion and Indian Popular Cinema

There are many religions in India, including Hinduism, Islam, Christianity, Buddhism and Jainism but the vast majority of Indian films that have a religious theme are Hindu in outlook. D.J. Phalke, the originator of Indian cinema, based his first feature film, *Raja Harischandra*, on a Hindu religious story, after he saw a film about the life of Christ. We noted how Indian filmmakers were from the start drawn to the *Ramayana* and the *Mahabharata* for stories, characters, ethos and values and this still continues. Religion and cinema are inseparably linked in Indian culture. However, religion in India is a highly sensitive issue and, according to Madan (1989), 'to write about it without querying the idea of religion as a discrete element of everyday life is to yield to the temptation of words'.

To what extent is an understanding of the religious traditions of India necessary to an appreciation of its cinema? We concentrate on the dominant religion, Hinduism, since Hindu religious traditions and practices mark the content, structure and dominant moods of Indian films generally. The relationship of Hinduism to Islam in particular and its impact on the film industry and the content of films needs also to be understood.

Sanatana Dharma – The Eternal Law

The eternal law governs the evolution of the individual from conception to death and to live in harmony with the laws of Nature herself. The traditional vision of life is holistic and this is the first principle for any understanding of religion in India. This vision of life encompasses almost every kind of religious belief and practice from pagan superstitions to scholarly traditions. However, some of the core concepts of Hinduism can be identified. These concepts include *karma, dharma, maya,* rebirth and renunciation.

As we noted earlier, at the heart of Hinduism is *dharma* – the Cosmic Moral Social order. The *Mahabharata* (C.400 BC – 400 AD) says '*Dharma* is so called because it protects *dharmat* (everything). *Dharma* maintains everything that has been created; *dharma* is thus that very principle which can maintain the universe' (Madan, 1989). This is comparable to the Christian 'Word', as in the Biblical: 'In the beginning was the Word, and the Word was with God and the Word was God'. There is, however, a significant difference in the ontological assumptions, since Hindus never contemplated the universe as a perfect system, governed by general laws.

Dharma, then, is a metaphysical concept, embracing as it does the abstract principle of the social order. It has, however, practical consequences – namely, 'the obligation and the tendency to act in a particular way in specified situations. The synthesis of thought and practice is even more clearly expressed in the notion of *karma*' (Madan, 1989: 122) – every action has its inevitable consequences. A person's life is determined by the good deeds and the bad deeds that s/he has performed in previous lives.

The concept of *karma* is closely linked to the idea of rebirth and seeks to explain the sufferings and hardships that one has to encounter in everyday life. Although the concept of *karma*, as enunciated in classical Indian texts, is highly complex, touching on philosophical and moral issues in the popular mind, it has been simplified to mean that some people are rich and others are poor, some people are healthy and others are not, because of their *karma*, their past deeds. The concept of *dharma*, as formulated in traditional texts, is equally complex and deals with issues of social order, law, religious sanctions, morality, duties and obligations and so on. However, in the popular imagination it has been simplified to mean the maintenance of the social order and the acceptance of one's prescribed life and the performance of one's duties accordingly. The notion of *maya*, as understood by the public and as portrayed in Indian films, is that the world is illusory. A veil is drawn between human beings and reality, and that veil constitutes *maya*. This is again tied to the concepts of *samsara* and *moksha* (liberation). So long as human beings fail to realise that the phenomenal world is illusory and that there is a deeper and real world of the inner self, they will be caught in the never-ending cycle of rebirth and fail to achieve liberation. The idea of rebirth is central to the Hindu view of life. Human beings are born again and again until they realise the deeper reality of life. The human soul remains the same, but it takes on and discards many bodily shapes. As the famous Hindi text, the *Bhagavad Gita*, states:

> As a man casts off his worn-out clothes
> And takes on other new ones in their place,
> So does the embodied soul cast off his worn-out bodies
> And enters others new.

The idea of renunciation is also central to the Hindu view of life and finds expression in many Indian films. According to the Hindus, there are four stages in a person's life. First a student, second a householder, third a hermit and fourth a holy man or one who has renounced worldly life for the quest of truth. Renunciation is thus a highly prized virtue. Watching Indian films with these concepts in mind enables us to understand the intentions of the filmmakers better and also the deeper layers of meanings embedded in the narratives.

Religious Explicitness

The relationship of these key concepts of Hinduism to Indian cinema can be studied at different levels. Firstly, there are films which are explicitly religious in nature, drawing their stories from religious sources, most notably the *Mahabharata* and the *Ramayana*. For example, the story of Rama and Sita – the abduction of Sita by the cruel demon-king Ravana, the eventual defeat of Ravana and the establishment of the purity of Sita find repeated expression in Indian cinema. An early example is *Lanka Dahan* (Lanka Aflame, 1933). Secondly, there are films that deal with the lives and futures of religious saints. Thirdly, there are many films that deploy religious concepts and images as a way of investing the stories with greater significance. Fourthly, there are films that portray different religious cults. Fifthly, we find works of Indian cinema that seek to critique various religious institutions, practices and religiosities.

Among films depicting the lives and fortunes of saints is the already mentioned *Sant Tukaram*, made in 1936. The seventeenth century Maharashtra saint Tukaram willingly accepts the sufferings and atrocities heaped upon him by his oppressor, the Brahmin Salamalo, who falsely claims to be the true author of Tukaram's songs. In the end he is vindicated and triumphant. This film struck a chord with those who were turning away from the dominance of Sanskrit towards the vernaculars and the domination of the Brahmin caste.

Sant Tulsidas, made in 1939, is another. Tulsidas is well-known as the author who rewrote the original *Valmiki Ramayana*. To the utter dismay of his teacher, the poet spends his time with his beloved, Ratnavali. However, suddenly, and happily for everyone concerned, Tulsidas discovers his life's vocation during a storm. He becomes an ascetic and settles down in Benares to work on his translation. There has even been a film about a female saint, Sakhu. *Sant Sakhu*, made in 1945, recounts the life of a devoutly religious woman. She is married and is subjected to humiliations and hardships by her in-laws, until a series of miracles makes people realise that she is a saint.

Films dealing with the life of saints still continue to be made – *Adi Shankaracharya* (1983) by G.V Iyer is particularly interesting. The first film made in Sanskrit, it is set in Kerala in the eighth century and tells the story of Shankara, the best known Advaita Vedanta philosopher. Over three hundred Sanskrit texts are attributed to him. The film opens with Shankara as a boy, living in a village and being introduced to the Brahmanical rituals. After the death of his father, the boy is drawn towards philosophy, which he sees as a way of coming to grips with the mysteries of life. He leads the life of a mendicant and spends his time studying religious texts. He has little interest in marriage and leads 'a household life'. He tells his mother that he would remain a devoted son while leading the life of a mendicant scholar. His teacher entrusts him with the task of writing new commentaries to ancient religious texts at which he excels. He becomes an ascetic and travels to the Himalayas. By now he has a reputation as a man of learning. The film shows how by the age of thirty-two he succeeds in transcending all early illusions and becoming one with the Ultimate. Iyer made two other saint films, one about Madhavacharya (1986) and one about Shri Ramanujacharya (1989).

G.V Iyer's latest film is a cinematic representation of the *Bhagavad Gita* (1992). Asked why he chose this text for cinematic presentation, Iyer explained: 'The Gita is not just about the war, about Krishna talking to Arjun. It deals with the evolution of man and the teachings and the laws which were bestowed upon him, informing him about all the characteristics which are found in man. And how he has to conquer evil and reach the goal of self-realisation'. Clearly, he sees it as a text with a universally valid message.

Some of these 'saint' films have had a profound influence on the thought and imagination of a good many people. For example the film *Jai Santoshi Ma*, made in 1975 by Sharma, was instrumental in transforming a little-known goddess into a popular icon. She attained a wide acceptance among modern working class women toiling in the cities. Satyavati is the foremost disciple of the goddess Santoshi on earth. When Satyavati marries Birju, the wives of the three deities Brahma, Vishnu and Shiva become terribly jealous and create a series of problems and crises to test her faith and devotion. She emerges triumphantly from these tests and with her faith shining as ever, so she is admitted to the godly pantheon. Films dealing with the lives of saints deserve careful study as we pursue the interrelationships between religion and cinema in India.

Religious Symbolism in Film

The third category of religious films includes all those in which religious symbols, concepts and images play a key role in framing the narrative and investing it with meaning. As we look back on the evolution of Indian poetry, drama, sculpture, painting and so on, we see that religious concepts and images have been at the heart of the communicated experience. Even in films with no overt connection to religion in terms of plot or character, the imprint of religious ideas and images can be seen. Take an example from the work of popular film director Raj Kapoor – who cannot be described as a maker of religious films. He was primarily interested in producing popular romantic musicals that were secular in outlook but he nonetheless uses religious concepts to structure the narrative and give it a clearer focus. His film *Satyam Shivam Sundaram* made in 1978, focuses on the virtues of love, truth and beauty, the transforming power of love and its capacity to illuminate truth and genuine beauty. Like his other films, this one deals with romantic love through song and dance, but it consciously makes use of religious ideas to enhance the story.

The film *The Ritual* (1977) by Girish Kasaravalli provides another example. It has as its structuring device a Brahmanic ritual called 'ghattashraddha' through which Brahmin widows were excommunicated. The film relates how Yamuna, the young widowed daughter of a Brahmin scholar, is seduced by a school teacher and made pregnant. The close-knit Brahmin community is outraged and the father of Yamuna decides to perform the ritual 'ghatashraddha' himself. Her head shaved, she is abandoned by the community. To be cast into widowhood is tantamount to falling from divine grace. To enjoy life as a widow is a sinful act which is irredeemable. Accordingly, anyone guilty of such acts is excommunicated through this ritual, which simulates the rituals of death on a living person. Indian cinema has produced many such films that are not religious but in which religious concepts are a way of organising the narrative.

Religious Cults and Institutions

A fourth category are the films that deal with specific religious cults, such as *Jai Santoshi Ma* (Santoshi Ma be praised!) or *Ishanou* (The Chosen One, 1990). The latter, made by Sharma, depicts the Meitei cult prevalent in Manipuri in India, inciting female adherents to join it by certain mystical powers that send them signals they cannot ignore. *Ishanou* is about a family that lives peacefully and happily in the Manipuri valley under the protection and care of an old woman. All of a sudden, the young wife Tampha becomes possessed by the deity Maibi and she leaves her home to be an active participant in the Maibi sect. The film contains exotic dances and rituals that illustrate for us the power of this religious cult.

Finally, films have, from the start, provided critiques of religious institutions, practices and understandings. Some have sought to point out the inequities of untouchability from the perspective of an enlightened humanism. More recently Satyajit Ray's *Devi* (Goddess, 1960) is notable and is discussed here in the section on women in Indian popular cinema. *Samskara* (Funeral Rites, 1970), also discussed in this book, reveals the dilemmas created by adhering too closely and rigidly to religious traditions. Questions of orthodoxy in religion are pitted against the changing social circumstances in a way that raises questions about the role of religious traditions in society.

Buddhist and Sikh Themes

The five categories discussed here relate to Hinduism, but a few films have been made in India that deal with other religions. *Angulimal* (1960) directed by Bhatt, is based on a well-known Buddhist story. Angulimal is a ruthless robber. He is called Angulimal because he wears a garland of human fingers cut from his victims' hands. He engages in bloody and cruel rituals in order to acquire divine powers. He encounters Buddha and sees the futility of his actions, repents for his past misdeeds and decides to follow the compassionate teachings of the Buddha. Here we find the confrontation of forces of light and darkness, creativity and destruction within a Buddhist philosophy.

Quoting extensively from the venerated Sikh text, the Granth Sahib, *Naanak Nam Jahaz Hai* (1969) explores aspects of a Sikh religious experience and seeks to capture the teachings of Guru Nanak. It narrates the story of Gurumukh Singh and his son Gurumeet. Gurumukh treats his partner Prem Singh as a younger brother until a business dispute ends their friendship. Prem Singh's wife wants her son Gurumeet to marry her niece Channi. During an argument she accidentally blinds him. Channi, the blind Gurumeet, and the repentant wife of Prem Singh set out on a pilgrimage of atonement, visiting all the Sikh shrines. Their troubled relationships are ultimately resolved at the famous Golden Temple in Amritsar. There, in response to Channi's prayers, a miracle takes place and Gurumeet's eyesight is restored.

Morality and Modernism

The relationship between religion and cinema in India can usefully be studied at another level also. Most of the films belong to the popular tradition of filmmaking and can be described as morality plays, where the forces of good and bad vie for supremacy. Plots are simple and little effort is made to portray complex human characters. In the contest between justice and injustice, light and darkness, wisdom and ignorance, the forces of justice, light and wisdom win out. What is interesting is that the movie-going public responds to them in the language and vocabulary of religious experiences, as Dissanayake and Sahai (1992) found when they interviewed hundreds of people in and around Delhi about such an extremely popular film as *Sholay*. People used expressions like 'It's all a matter of fate', 'God's will prevails in the end', 'The world was created with a purpose, and goodness has to triumph', 'What we see here is the action of karma', 'If you are devoted to God, no harm will come to you', 'One has to know one's dharma' and so on. The majority of film-goers in India look for morals in films and the power of God to set right injustice. The language in which they express these wishes is coloured by religious sentiments and religious convictions and merits closer study here.

India, like most other countries, is caught up in the process of modernisation. Some parts of the country are modernising at a faster pace than the others, but no region is unaffected. What this means is that questions of rationality, secularism, individuality, science and technology are foregrounded as never before. As a consequence one sees in modern Indian films – certainly those in the artistic tradition, but increasingly in popular films also – a conflict between religious values and modernising values. Some present this conflict as one between Westernisation and tradition – mistakenly. The real contest is between religious values and secular values, as films associated with the

New Indian Cinema demonstrate. So when we explore the topic of religion and cinema in India we need to pay close attention to this ongoing, and ever-increasing, contest between religious and secular values.

In modern Indian films, as opposed to many of the earlier films, one sees the emergence of a new kind of self as embodied in the character of the protagonist. This is certainly true of artistic films, but even in certain popular films such as Mani Rathnam's *Bombay* (1994), we can see this. Through the character of the journalist Shekhar, we see emerging a self which is secular, modern, suspicious of undue veneration of the past and desirous of bringing about ethnic and religious tolerance. A kind of liberal humanism pervades the outlook of these new heroes. We need to examine the nature and significance of such new thinking against the backdrop of religious belief in India to understand not only Indian cinema and its evolution but also some important aspects of Indian society and culture. Many cultural critics see this shift as significant in light of the fierce conflicts between religious groups which seem to tear apart the Indian social fabric.

In addition to the different and complex ways in which religious thought finds expression in Indian cinema and the contradictory pulls of religious and secular values in more recent films, gifted Indian filmmakers display cinematic sensibility to religious sentiments and symbols. G.Aravindan's *Chidambaram* (1985) is representative. Set on a commercial farm, the characters are not securely anchored to a solid and stable social order deriving sustenance from tradition, but are uprooted and transplanted into an artificial setting where they have to cultivate their individual selves.

Chidambaram deals with the complex relationships among four characters. Shankaran is an office superintendent on a farm located on the border of Kerala and Tamil Nadu. Jacob is a field supervisor, deeply conscious of his duties as well as the authority invested in him. Although their friendship is close, they are very different characters. Shankaran, who lives by himself, is well-liked by his subordinates. Jacob is pragmatic and proud, conscious of social hierarchy and he is not unduly perturbed by questions of morality and ethics. Muniyandi, who works as a labourer on this farm, is meek, submissive and deeply religious. He goes back to the village to get married and Shankaran, who is an amateur photographer, attends the wedding to take pictures. Shivagami, Muniyandi's wife, comes to live on the farm. She, like the rest of the characters in this film, is uprooted from her village environment and compelled to live in the artificial setting of the farm. At first she is totally overwhelmed by the strangeness, lushness and beauty of her new environment. The film shows beautifully, through carefully framed and vivid images, how she adjusts and comes to terms with her new surroundings. Shankaran becomes friendly with Shivagami, finding her extraordinarily gentle and attractive.

One day, Jacob comments in jest on Shankaran's interest in Shivagami, upsetting Shankaran, who hits him. Later he questions himself regarding his strange and inexplicable behaviour. Meanwhile, Jacob is trying hard to find employment for Shivagami on the farm. Muniyandi disapproves of the idea, but Shivagami is bored with doing nothing and eager to find work on the farm. Jacob finds her a job but Muniyandi, suspicious of Jacob's motives, turns down the offer. Jacob, annoyed and insulted, orders Muniyandi to work on the night shift. Muniyandi, overcome by growing suspicion, listens carefully to every sound as he works. One night, he hears a motorcycle making its way towards the house. In great anxiety, he rushes to the house and sees the shadow of a man slipping out of the back door. To his utter astonishment, it is not Jacob, as he had suspected, but his trusted supervisor Shankaran.

Early next morning, Muniyandi is found to have committed suicide. Shattered by this unexpected turn of events, Shankaran flees the farm and his life is transformed by the implacable power of guilt. He becomes an alcoholic, living a rootless existence in an artificial environment without the support of a stable community that he would find in a typical village and with no one to turn to. Shankaran wanders aimlessly; the doctor who treats him suggests that he immerses himself in religious texts and goes on holiday to places of religious significance. Shankaran starts to wander again and ends up at the famous Chidambaram temple. After visiting it, he pauses to put on his shoes and pay the haggard-looking woman who watches over them at the entrance. As she lifts up her face, Shankaran at once recognises Shivagami. He notes a deep scar on her face, probably indicating that Muniyandi beat her before he took his own life. Clearly, Shankaran has come to the end of his journey.

Chidambaram is the famous Hindu temple in South India where Lord Shiva was supposed to have been transformed into the famed cosmic dancer who enables human beings to free themselves from their earthiness and ex-perience supramundane reality. The marvellously effective final sequence of the film takes place at the temple where, with imaginative camera work and accompanying thandava music, the earthly and supramundane levels of the film meet in exquisite union.

Aravindan, who has always been interested in exploring modes of religious and mythic consciousness in his films, is here introducing a metaphysical dimension. We have discussed this film at some length because it illustrates how even in films that do not deal with religious subjects or experiences, a religious sensibility operating on the creativity of the director can have intriguing results. There are many Indian films that manifest this tendency.

The emergence of a pronounced secular self in modern Indian society and cinema that is responding to the forces of modernisation, does not mean that religion has been eliminated from contemporary society. On the contrary, it has become an increasingly vital force. The rise of Hindu fundamentalism in India, like the rise of Muslim, Jewish or Christian fundamentalisms in other parts of the world, has taken most scholars by surprise. Why was the significant role that religion would assume in public life in most societies not predicted? Was a simple antagonism between religion and modernity posited, with insufficient attention paid to the complex and multi-faceted ways in which they interact? Was the notion of modernity too simplistic to become a useful analytical tool in understanding the interplay of religion and society? These and similar questions are being heard today. What the latest writings on the subject seem to suggest is that religion did not disappear under the onslaught of modernisation; it merely relocated itself.

Daniel Bell explains the place of religion in modern society in terms of two separate causal chains: secularisation and profanation. He saw secularisation as the disengagement of religion from the public sphere and political life and religion as retreating into a private world. However, in the contemporary world, the exact opposite seems to have taken place. Religion is at the centre of the public sphere and political life. Many thoughtful filmmakers in India, as elsewhere, are beginning to question the received wisdoms about religion and society. In addition, we are seeing the increasing commodification of religious institutions and practices. Buying and selling mystical powers associated with religion is on the rise. A link between religion and profit-making is not new, but it has become far more widespread and international in outlook. Instant gurus, quacks, and charlatans give religion a bad name. All this does not go unnoticed by the more independent-minded filmmakers.

This broad review of religion in Indian cinema has indicated the valuable insights it affords into Indian society and Indian cinema. A study of a religion is also a study of the culture in which that religion flourishes. In the case of Islam, for example, although the central teachings may be universal, the ways in which they find cultural articulation differ according to the culture in which they are rooted, so Islam in India is not identical to Islam in Saudi Arabia or Iraq or Indonesia. The relationship between religion and society is evolving in India just as much as the representation of religion in cinema is evolving.

The Influence of the Cinema in the South of India

Although Bombay is usually considered the capital of the Indian film world, 'the film industry in the South, centred in Madras, is the largest in India in terms of the number of studios, capital investment, gross income and in the number of people engaged in the industry' (Hardgrave, 1975).

The glitter and excitement associated with Bombay is replaced in Madras by intense feeling for linguistic identity together with the promotion of the Dravidian Tamil heritage and this has led to cinema being used for political propaganda. In 1944, Annadurai founded the Dravida Munnetra Kazhagam (DMK) which eventually led to the downfall of the Congress Party in Madras and the election of Annadurai as the first DMK Chief Minister of Tamilnadu.

However, it was the spectacular rise of M.G.Ramchandran (MGR), N.T.Rama Rao (NTR) and Jayalalitha and the 'divine' powers attributed to them by their fans which turned them into starry politicians. In his films, MGR saw himself as the 'protector' of the common man and he is convinced of the moral purpose of his films: 'My roles have been to show how a man should live and believe'. Mother tongue, motherland and motherhood were the stuff on which MGR's popularity was founded. 'Backed by a powerful party, aided by one million fan clubs spread all over the state, he became the Chief Minister of Tamilnadu in the 1970s and stayed in power for ten years.' (Garga 1996:269). Garga gives an example of the emotional response that MGR could evoke 'when in 1987 during a critical illness, 22 people committed suicide in the hope that their deaths would somehow save their leader' (Garga 1996:269).

The same adulation is given to NTR and Jayalalitha. NTR played the mythological Gods, Rama and Krishna, in over 100 feature films and his fans deified him as the Omnipotent, the Omniscient and Omnipresent. Jayalalitha not only succeeded MGR as the Chief Minister, but was also an enormously influential actress. At the height of her acting career, she received huge numbers of letters from her fans, some requesting her to send her photo to cure illnesses. Her supporters have committed bizarre acts, prostrating themselves before her or 'rolling on the streets to show their devotion to her'. (Garga 1996:270). As Hardgrave (1975) rightly observes, star worship represents a cathartic identification: 'the world of the film star becomes a repository of displaced frustration. The star provides the avenue of escape from the tedium of everyday life, from the desperation of poverty'.

Ethnicity and Caste

In recent years the concept of ethnicity has gained intellectual respectability, particularly through the development of Cultural Studies. Issues of ethnicity, identity and the problem of minorities are crucially linked. Ethnicity is difficult to define precisely but an ethnic group can be described as a self-conscious collection of people united, or closely related, by characteristics acquired at birth (colour, for example) and/or by culturally shared experiences such as language, religion and caste.

Hindu-Muslim Conflict

When we talk about ethnicity and the problems of minorities in India, the conflict between Hindus and Muslims comes immediately to mind. After the partitioning of India in 1947, most Muslims settled in the newly formed state of Pakistan but to today there are over one hundred million Muslims living in India. Periodically, open and often violent conflicts occur between Hindus and Muslims in India. A number of filmmakers have sought to focus on this issue in their work and three films that deal with the Hindu-Muslim conflict in India are now briefly discussed.

The first is by Hindu filmmaker M.S.Sathyu. *Garam Hava* (Hot Winds, 1975) narrativises the collective brutal violence against the Muslims during partition. To dramatise this violence on screen Sathyu has focused on the misfortunes and privations of a single family. Salim Mirza (superbly played by Balraj Sahni) is a shoe manufacturer whose family has lived in Agra for generations. With partition in 1947, Mirza, like thousands of other Muslims, was faced with the unpalatable choice of leaving India for the newly created state of Pakistan or stay and incurring the collective hostilities of the Hindu majority in India. His elder brother, Halim a shrewd politician, resolves to leave India, but Mirza will not. In his bones, he feels that India is his country and he wants to remain behind and continue with the family business. As Salim Mirza's daughter Amina is engaged to Halim's son Kazim, the situation becomes more complicated. The border between India and Pakistan is closed off, and Kazim is prohibited from coming back to meet his bride. He succeeds after much effort in crossing the border illegally and preparations are hastily made for the wedding, but the police show up and Kazim is apprehended.

The agonies and hardships resulting from the partitioning begin to affect Mirza's life. He loses his business, and his daughter commits suicide. The film conveys Mirza's miseries honestly and movingly, if a little sentimentally. At last after much agonising, he decides to accept the inevitable and leave

India with his son. As they make their way to the railway station for their departure, they find themselves among a procession of protesters of diverse social, political, religious, ethnic affiliations. All of them belong to marginalised and disenfranchised groups. Mirza abandons his plans to leave the country and joins the protesters in the hope that their clamour will awaken the people to the mindless violence around them and make public opinion more enlightened.

In *Garam Hava* director Sathyu has highlighted the plight of Muslims in India with sympathy and understanding. A Hindu himself, he has sought to promote a keener appreciation of the difficulties and hardships encountered by minorities. The film reminds us that the nation of India is made up of diverse ethnic, linguistic, religious groups and that the rights of each of the group need to be protected. *Garam Hava* is a good example of how the camera helps us to share the humdrum daily living of 'ordinary' families: people make tea, the father reads a newspaper, the mother sews a dress and a young girl sits on a bed trying on bangles, while the bangle-seller woman sits on the floor. As we feel the web of relations holding members of the family together, we share their pain as this web disintegrates under the strain of partition. Khanna (1980) has provided a detailed reading of Garam Hava. One of his central points is that although the film 'fails to analyse the causes either of the partition or the sufferings undergone by individuals', it vividly depicts the daily lives in a Muslim household to people in India who have had only slight acquaintance with Muslims.

The second film that deals with the Hindu-Muslim conflict is Saeed Akhtar Mirza's *Salim Langde Pe Mat Ro* (Don't Cry for Salim the Lame, 1989). It centres on the life and fortunes of Salim, a young Muslim attempting to carve out an identity for himself in a hostile world. Salim is poor and leads a life of crime, his role models being racketeers and smugglers who have achieved material success by brazenly defying the law; his sought-after world pays little respect to moral values. He lives in a world of poverty, moral degrada-tion, crime and violence. If Salim represents 'the self-destructive element among Muslim youth, his counterpoint is provided by Aslam, highly educated and idealistic, who can find no job other than that of a low-paid proof reader' (Garga 1996:257). Although Salim tries to embrace a more compassionate view of life, the operative logics of his social world would have none of it. In the midst of celebrations for his sister's wedding, Salim is knifed to death by a member of a rival gang.

In *Don't Cry for Salim the Lame*, the intention of the director is to focus attention on the Muslims in India, especially those living in the cities. The film has as its theme the question of belonging and unbelonging in modern India, and how the nation-state can marginalise the minorities in most unsatisfactory ways. The director has underlined the need to take very seriously the problems and hardships of the Muslim minority if gratuitous violence is to be avoided.

The third film dealing with this complicated and troubled relationship (and mentioned earlier) is by the Hindu filmmaker Mani Rathnam. It is more recent and it generated heated debate in India and even assassination attempts. *Bombay* (1994) deals with forbidden love, against the backdrop of Hindu-Muslim conflict. The story centres around the love between a Hindu journalist and a Muslim girl whose parents are implacably opposed to it. They run away to the city of Bombay and get married. They have two children and their parents begin to accept them. However, as things brighten up on the personal front, violence breaks out in Bombay as a consequence of the mounting tensions between Hindus and Muslims.

Mani Rathnam is careful not to favour either the Hindu or the Muslim point of view but, as was to be expected, the film was highly controversial and led to protests from both communities. In fact, *Bombay* encapsulates many of the issues regarding the cultural differences between Hindus and Muslims and their representation in films. It is time that the sectarian violence and the incidents which wrought havoc in Bombay in 1992/1993 were used in film as part of the narrative. The dichotomy between the village and the city (discussed earlier, particularly in our analysis of the films of the 1950s) is again emphasised but in a different light – inter-communal conflict in the village as against the city. Over the past 40 years, Indian popular cinema has almost always highlighted the Hindu hero; here, however, the character of the Hindu journalist is there for Mani Rathnam to argue for a more enlightened attitude towards the relationship between Hindus and Muslims. Mani Rathnam is following previous film directors in search of harmony among the communities and shows that there are no winners in the inhumanity of communal strife. The filmmaker, through the character of the Hindu journalist, pleads for rational thinking and a more enlightened attitude. These three films, in their different ways and from their distinctive vantage points, are among a number that have dealt with this issue.

The Parsis

Muslims are only one minority in India, The Parsis are another. Followers of prophet Zoroaster and descendants of Persian Zoroastrians, they immigrated to India in the eighth century to avoid religious persecution by the Muslims.

They are a commercially successful ethnic group who are known for their wealth as well as their beneficence and constitute an important subculture of India. Since establishing themselves in India as a distinct ethnic group they have contributed significantly to the commercial, scientific and artistic life of the country. *Pestonjee* (1987), directed by Vijaya Mehta, seeks to capture an aspect of the complex reality of the Parsis. The film deals with the culture, way of life and conventions that govern the social life of the influential Parsi community of India. The human drama captured in this film gains depth and definition from the dynamics of this subculture. The film presents the life of Piroj and his deep friendship with Pesi. Mehta has expanded on a short story by B.K.Karanjia in a way that allows her to probe the characters more comprehensively.

Pirojshau (Piroj) and Pestonjee (Pesi) are close friends and bachelors. Some-one suggested to Piroj that he marry Jeroo, a girl of romantic dreams. But characteristically Piroj cannot decide immediately and meanwhile, Pesi agrees to marry her. Once Pesi is a married man, the relationship between Piroj and Pesi undergoes certain changes. Piroj is transferred to the town of Bhusaval and the marital relationship between Pesi and Jeroo is subject to various strains. Piroj receives a letter from Pesi informing him that Jeroo is expecting a baby; filled with joy, Piroj resolves to visit them. On his arrival, he realises that things are not bright and happy as he had expected. Pesi had begun to have an affair and Piroj disapproves. Pesi resents his friend's desire to run his life. The two friends drift apart, vowing never to meet again.

Three years pass. Unexpectedly, Piroj receives a New Year card from Pesi, intimating that he misses Piroj greatly. Meanwhile, Piroj is transferred to Bombay and the two friends meet briefly and try, with little success, to revive their friendship. The following morning Pesi dies of a heart attack. Summarised in this fashion, *Pestonjee* may appear somewhat sentimental and there is certainly a strain of sentimentality in the film. But it is counter-balanced by the comic observations of the director and the humour generated by the dialogue as well as the acting. From our point of view, what is interesting about this film is the way the three main characters are securely situated in the Parsi sub-culture and how the customs, beliefs, rituals, values associated with the Parsis frame the entire experience.

The Theme of Ethnicity

Ethnicity figures in other interesting ways in Indian cinema. In popular films, ethnic stereotypes are sometimes presented for comic effect. Indeed, the link between Sanskrit drama and popular cinema continues through familiar and sometimes well-paid comedians. According to Valicha (1988:73), a comic interlude has been traditionally regarded as an essential feature of every popular film. Each comedian specialises in a certain type of comic ability: Johnny Walker evoking a rustic element, Gope the witless fool, Mehmood an earthy and sensual humour. The comic characters are very often visually different from the heroes; for example, Mukri, who is short and slow witted.

Occasionally the need is stressed for ethnic harmony and authenticity. As Valicha (1988,75) put it: 'while the film in its totality perpetuates an apparently false world of artifice and luxury, the comic seems to break that overbearing illusion and pour out, in a bucolic and homely manner, affirmations of everyday life. It seems to give the film a ring of authenticity'. At other times, national unity is stressed with great sentimentality. For example in *Amar, Akbar, Anthony* (1977) which tells the story of a Hindu, a Muslim and a Christian, the joy of national unity and inter-ethnic harmony is celebrated.

Whether this is rhetoric or reality very often depends on the national and the international situation. For example, the fluctuating relationship between India and Pakistan over the Kashmir issue, the campaign to establish Khalistan and the rise of Hindu nationalism have dented the fabric of a multi-religious India. What happens to India will largely depend on how powerful Hindu nationalism becomes – for example, the influence of Bal Thackaray's Shiv Shena in Maharastra. And this in turn will have serious consequences on the Indian cinema, where inter-ethnic harmony has always been celebrated.

The Asian Diaspora

Different notions of ethnicity emerge when we consider ethnic minorities settled abroad. For example, until recently the Asian perspective in British film culture has generally been excluded. There have been quite a number of Asian film-makers working in Britain (e.g. Waris Hussain, Jamil Dehlavi, Ismail Merchant) who did not present the Asian experience. It could even be argued that they confirmed the West's fascination with the Orient, the exotic, in films such as *Gandhi, A Passage to India, Heat and Dust, Jewel in the Crown*, in which the nostalgia of the 'Raj' is reworked. In his insightful article 'Locating the Asian Experience', Perminder Dhillon-Kashyap (1988) comments:

> These nostalgic tales of the 'Raj' reiterate and intensify the same colonial images – of the 'other', the 'darkie', the 'alien' – which were created and used to justify colonialism, while making a pretence of questioning the morality of imperialism. Thus beguiling the audience,

Salaam Bombay

implicit cultural discriminations are presented as 'truths'. Colonial atrocities by the British are then presented as deeds of extreme personalities (policeman Merrick in the *Jewel in the Crown* and Colonel Dyer in *Gandhi*).

Since the 1980s, however, there have been some Asian screenwriters and directors who have made an impact on the big and small screens. Hanif Kureishi's *My Beautiful Laundrette* (1985) received wide acclaim although his *Sammy and Rosie Get Laid* (1987) was less successful. Nair's *Salaam Bombay* (1988) is more of a documentary of dispossessed youth living on their wits in an uncaring city.

Nair's *Mississippi Masala* (1991) created a stir among the Asians because of its love affair between the Asian, Sarita Choudhury and the 'black' American, Denzel Washington. However, it was *Bhaji on the Beach* (1993) which caught the imagination of Asians in Britain. This is a 'tale of two generations of Asian women on a day trip to Blackpool and includes a Punjabi version of Summer Holiday' (*The Guardian* 15/11/96 p.5).

Caste

Ethnicity is one social division in India: another is caste where the division is found within the Hindu social order. No other institution in India has so exercised the imagination of foreigners as the caste system. It is highly complex, so has been frequently misinterpreted. The word 'caste' derives from the Portuguese word *casta* meaning colour – and colour forms an important part of the Indian caste system. Caste is basically a system of social classification, a mechanism by which people are grouped into traditionally sanctioned categories. All categorisations are based on certain accepted criteria. The concepts of purity and pollution are central to the Indian caste system. Behind it lies a complex world of classification – of things, actions and thoughts in terms of their relative purity and impurity and their relative power to pollute. Contact, either directly or obliquely, with things that are deemed impure results in pollution and has to be removed through various acts of ritual purification. This caste classification system has separated people in terms of professional activities – priests, landowners, merchants, cultivators, artisans, menials and so on.

The caste system originated with the Indo-European nomadic tribes generally known as Aryans, who made their way to India over thirty thousand years ago. These tribes originally came as pastoral raiders, but later merged with the indigenous population and settled down in India. Historians tell us that they came in distinct waves, the earliest arriving in India in about 1300 BC. Before long many of the non-Aryan tribes living in the country were Aryanized. The Aryan word for the native was 'dasa', which literally means slave, and this class was incorporated into the newly established Aryan social order called 'sudras' and with this amalgamation, a new social hierarchy emerged. Initially, there were four classes: Brahmin (priest), Kshatriya (warrior), Vaishya (trader) and Sudra (cultivator). This four-fold division gave rise to the elaborate caste system. Below the Sudras are the untouchables, often referred to as the 'Scheduled Castes'. Their extremely degraded status derived from their performing certain menial and dirty tasks. In recent years, many call themselves *dalits* (oppressed) and have revolted against their status.

Caste is an important institution in Indian society, which the rapid modernisation of Indian society has invested with much tension. Caste divisions have formed the backdrop of many Indian films, both popular and artistic, from the very beginning. *Achut Kanya* (1936) and *Sujata* (1959) for

Bhaji on the Beach

example, sought to alert public opinion about the ill-effects of caste distinctions. Bimal Roy's *Sujata* (1959) deals with the issue of caste in relation to romantic love and individual desire. Sujata is an untouchable. As an infant, she is taken care of by an engineer and his wife of the Brahmin caste. This arrangement is intended to be only temporary and it is assumed that suitable arrangements would be made. However, no home is found for her, and the family grows fond of her and raises her as a daughter. A marriage is arranged for their real daughter, Rama with Adhir, whose family becomes concerned that an untouchable girl is living with Rama's family. However, they resolve that the marriage should go ahead as planned and that Sujata should be married off to a suitable person. They insist that Sujata should not be present at Rama and Adhir's wedding. However, things do not work out as they anticipate. Adhir falls in love with Sujata and wants to marry her instead of Rama. Films like *Achut Kanya* and *Sujata* served to focus attention on how the caste system operates in India.

At times, the theme of caste is treated in terms not of inter-caste interactions but of the dynamics within one caste group. One example is *Samskara* (Funeral Rites, 1970), based on the widely discussed novel by U.R. Ananthamurthy. It deals with the inner workings of the close-knit community of Madhava Brahmins. One of the group is Naranappa, always a heretic who defied the accepted norms of behaviour. Having broken all the sacred codes of the Brahmins by eating meat, drinking, and keeping a mistress of low caste, Naranappa dies of plague. His death presents the Brahmins of this group with a problem: who will perform the final funeral rites for him? As long as the defiled body of Naranappa lies in his home, it is not possible for his family members or other Brahmins to eat or even have a drink of water. Any Brahmin who touched the body of Naranappa would be defiled. The film explores this predicament. *Achut Kanya*

The question of caste and its ramifications finds expression not only in popular cinema but also in artistic films, for example, Satyajit Ray's *Sadgati*

(*Deliverence*), made for television in 1981. Based on a short story by the celebrated Hindi writer Premchand, the film explores how the discourse of caste intersects with other important social institutions and practices. Pandit Ghashiram is a powerful Brahmin priest who lives in a small village and performs sacrificial ceremonies and advises the villagers about auspicious and inauspicious times. In this village lives a poor untouchable by the name of Dukhi. His daughter is about to get married, and he wants Pandit Ghashiram to help him select an auspicious date for his daughter's wedding. Pandit Ghashiram promises to help him and Dukhi agrees to do manual labour for him in return. Dukhi is asked to chop an old trunk of a tree into small pieces with an axe. The wood is hard and he fails to cut the tree trunk. He is exhausted and longs to smoke his clay pipe. As he has no matches to light, he goes into Pandit Ghashiram's house to ask the wife of Pandit Ghashiram for some charcoal. She is outraged; she cannot believe that an untouchable dare enter her house. Dukhi goes back and starts to chop down the tree. He collapses and dies and, in this predominantly Brahmin village, the corpse of an untouchable lying there becomes a public nuisance.

Satyajit Ray portrays these events in a way that brings out the meaning of duty and caste system as well as questions of exploitation, tradition, modernity, and private and public morality. These same issues are explored from a different angle in Ghosh's *Antarjali Yatra* (The Voyage Beyond, 1987). Although sati is the dramatic core of the film (see Rajadhyaksha and Willemen, 1994:443 for an outline of the plot), the close physical proximity between the 'untouchable' Baiju and the Brahmin's bride awakens the latter's sexuality. The setting is a cremation ground and Ghosh uses the camera to bring the scenes remarkably to life through light, space, motion and colour. At the same time, Ghosh delivers a powerful blow to tradition and the caste system.

In India's multi-racial, multi-religious society, social issues connected with ethnic conflicts and ethnic strife are inevitably explored by Indian film-makers. Hinduism is the predominant religion in India, and the Hindu religion sets great store by the caste system. As India, like all societies, is subject to modernisation, the caste system becomes challenged by notions of equality, citizenship and democratic participation. Many filmmakers sensitive to such issues find the caste system an important site in which to examine social issues vital to India.

CHAPTER 5

Women in Indian Cinema

The complex and fascinating relationship between women and cinema has a substantial literature and there is some interesting work on Third World feminism, which illuminates aspects of the representation of women in Indian films.

Here, we focus attention on two areas: the representation *of* women and the representation *by* women on screen. Both aspects are essential for understanding the interplay between women and cinema in India. It is useful to deal first with the representation of women in the popular and artistic cinema, referring to a number of illustrative examples.

The Representation of Women on the Screen

In traditional Indian society, there were definite and consensual norms of behaviour – that regulated the conduct of women – all of them handed down from the past. For example, the concept of woman as *Sita* is prevalent in Indian society as well as Indian films. *Sita*, immortalised in the *Ramayana*, is the ideal woman, the ideal wife; she is steadfastly loyal to her husband and obeys his wishes unquestioningly. The *Ramayana* says that a wife's god is her husband: he is her friend, her teacher. Her life is of less consequence than her husband's happiness. Over the years, Indian popular cinema had perpetuated this ideal of a wife's selfless devotion.

In traditional Indian society, the lives of women were severely circumscribed. Strict rules and regulations had to be followed. Women's roles were essentially as daughter (Beti), wife (Patni) and mother (Ma). According to the *Manusmriti*, which had a profound effect on shaping the morals of Indian society, a female should be subject in childhood to her father, in youth to her husband, and when her husband is dead, to her children. Women were given no kind of independence. *Manusmriti* is emphatic that a woman must not strive to separate herself from her father, her husband, her sons. She is told to be always cheerful, efficient in the management of household affairs, fastidious in cleaning utensils, careful with expenses. She is expected to be unwaveringly obedient to her husband, and after he is dead she must make every effort to honour his memory. These norms governed the lives of women in traditional India, and they find clear articulation in Indian cinema, especially in popular films.

Not that romantic love was prohibited for women. If that were the case, many popular Indian films would not have been made. Women were permitted to indulge in romantic love if it followed the *Radha-Krishna* model. In classical Indian texts, the love of *Radha* for *Krishna* is all-consuming, absolutely pure, and eternal and this is the kind of romantic love depicted in mainstream Indian films. Women who seek to live by the traditional norms find happiness, while those who dare to transgress them are punished and victimised, as a few representative examples will illustrate.

In *Do Anjane* (Two Strangers) made in the seventies, a woman who tries to defy the prescribed code of conduct is severely punished. This wife who wants to pursue a career as a classical Indian dancer is portrayed as self-centred and arrogant, causing her husband economic hardships and then leaving him. However, the husband she impoverished ultimately becomes rich and successful and highly esteemed by society, while she suffers all the indignities of a society that finds her a decadent woman.

Thodisi Bewafayi (1980) is another popular film with the same moral. The daughter (played by talented actress Shabana Azmi) of an indulgent father decides to marry the man with whom she is in love. Her husband loses his money and becomes poor. Instead of making use of her education, securing a job and improving the family fortunes, she resolves to go back to her father – but he too loses his job. She then goes to her brother's house, where her brother's wife begins to dislike her intensely. She ends up defeated, over-whelmed by misery and keen to go back to her husband.

However, there have always been films that challenge this treatment of women. For example, V. Shantaram's *Duniya Na Mane* (Uncompromising World, 1957), highly valued by Indian film historians, concerns an orphaned young woman who is tricked into marriage with an old man by her uncle who is greedy for money and who, with great strength of character, refuses to perform any of the wifely duties expected of her by society. The husband comes to realise the evils of his action as well as the injustices heaped upon women by society. In order to grant her the kind of freedom that she deserves, he takes his life.

Two roles that are of particular significance in Indian popular cinema are those of mother and wife, and there is a disparity between the representation of these two roles. It is a worldwide practice to think of one's country as one's 'motherland' but Indian reference to the mother is loaded with religious significance and the country is conflated with the mother goddess, Shakti (literally strength). The concept of the country as mother finds resonance in the national hymn *Vandemataran!* (Hail 'Mother (land)'), and the mother in Indian films is always revered as a vital force in society – as in *Mother India* (1957), which is in many ways the 'quintessential Indian film' (Thomas, 1989).

Yet although the wife is represented as a victim of social conventions and her individuality is severely limited, the word Shakti is used to describe her role as mother in Indian films. More appropriate to describe the wife may be the word Sati (extreme devotion to her husband). The Sati concept led to a considerable number of films in the 1920s and 1930s (e.g *Sati Parvati*, 1920; *Sati Anjani*, 1922; *Sati Ansuya*, 1933; *Sati Seeta*, 1924; *Sati Savitri*, 1927) and, although it is no longer fashionable, its effect was to portray women as stereotypical, unidimensional creatures with no personal ambitions of their own.

Nevertheless, this ideal wife *must* be sexually pure and the epitome of sexual fidelity. As Richards (1995) observes, the Hindi film upholds the 'traditional patriarchal views of society which, fearful of female sexuality, demands of the woman a subjugation of her desires' (p3). Consistent with the cultural norms pertaining to the status of women in Indian society, the honour of the family (Izzat) is closely linked to female behaviour. The need to preserve honour is expressed through 'elaborate, codified behaviour patterns that require the woman to remain secluded, confined to the domestic domain and dependent on the husband.'

The opposite of the wife is the vamp, normally a decadent modern woman, generally with a name like Rosie or Mary. She flouts tradition and seeks to imitate western women. She drinks, smokes, visits night clubs and is quick to fall in and out of love. She is portrayed as a morally degraded person and has come to be associated with everything that is unwholesome about the west. And she is almost always punished for her unacceptable behaviour. There is an interesting contradiction here. Indian cinema is a product of cultural modernity and it has accelerated the process of modernity in India as few other media have. Yet the woman who chooses to identify herself with modernity is almost always portrayed as decadent and punished for it.

Another frequent representation of womanhood in mainstream Indian cinema is the courtesan. The courtesan is commonly found in classical art and literature, ministering to the physical and emotional needs of men. The courtesan in Indian films is represented as existing outside the normal domain of domesticity and she is deeply attracted to the protagonist of the film, although usually he does not fall in love with her. She provides him with comfort, care, physical happiness and then, when he has adequately recovered from the miseries he has had to contend with and goes back to his sanctioned life, she pines for him. This theme, which was clearly established in such films as *Devdas* (1935), has continued to affect audiences. There have been films that contravene this pattern, such as *Chetna,* made in 1970 which tells the story of a young man who falls in love with a beautiful girl only to discover that she is a prostitute but is so attracted to her that he marries her.

Indian popular films are largely romantic musicals, and romance plays a significant role. The female protagonist is beautiful and the camera always makes a point of capturing her beauty in sensual detail. She becomes an object of male desire just as in American and European films. But the ways in which the female form is displayed in Indian popular films are culture-specific.

Kissing is a sensitive issue. In 'The State and Culture: Hindi cinema on the Passive Revolution' Prasad (1994) offers an illuminating discussion on the theme of kissing. According to Prasad, the prohibition of kissing scenes was based on an unwritten rule; the written rules 'prohibited excessively passionate love scenes', 'indelicate sexual situations' and 'scenes suggestive of immorality', all of which were derived from the British code of Censorship applied in Britain as well as (with modification) in British India' (ibid, p.173). Public kissing is associated with western life, so is alien to Indian culture. But the paradox is that the restrictions have never been applied in the censorship of foreign films. Furthermore, while the majority of the Indian audience as well as many notable film personalities would appear to favour the ban on scenes of kissing in Indian films, the vulgarity in the depiction of sexual activity in Indian films is transparent and this is difficult to reconcile with the ban on scenes of kissing.

How then is sexuality conveyed? The Indian cinema excels in the matter of disguised acts of sexual excitement by operating on the basis that the female form nude is less exciting than veiled. Richards (1995) has identified strategies used to display the female form and female sexual desire:

(a) **Tribal Dress** It is in the song and cabaret dance numbers that 'tribal costumes are used for the exposure of vast expanses of the body, in particular the pelvic region'. Richards (1995:5) notes that the short skirts, brief blouses and veil-less upper torso allow for maximum female exposure in Hindi films, that will not invite opprobrium from the nation's moral authorities.

(b) **Dream sequences/wet saris** A second device is the 'wet sari dance' which is, according to Richards (1995): 'legitimised by a sudden, torrential downpour that soaks the woman's flimsy sari, and allows for a very provocative and sexually tantalising exposure of the female body'. Allied to this device is the strategy of dream sequences. These dream sequences provide the freedom to indulge in the exploration of forbidden pleasures which include the display of the female body as well as the expression of sexual desire.

In *Deewana* (Madly in Love, 1967), Rishi Kapoor and Divyabharati fall in love and marry. Halfway through the film Rishi Kapoor is killed. When Shahrukh Khan sees his widow, he immediately falls in love with her. But as she is a grieving widow, she ignores his attentions. Dressed in white, her only activity is a daily visit to the temple. But Shahrukh Khan refuses to be discouraged by this and lying in bed, he drifts into a reverie and, in a dream sequence constructed around a song and dance number, he frolics with Divjabharati, now transformed into a modern, energetic woman.

(c) **Behind the Bush** The song and dance sequences often give rise to another strategy which allows the dancing couple to retreat behind a bush or a tree and after a pause the heroine emerges into the frame wiping her lips. Prasad (1994:177-178) presents this as 'a public confirmation of a private act which has cultural associations with a certain feudal practice of communal eroticism that consists of the display of the marks of sexual initiation on the female body'. Such erotic display of the female body in the popular cinema can be explained by the ideology of the public sphere. 'The female body as spectacle is a public representation, a putting before the public of an erotic imagery that does not violate the code that prohibits the representation of the private'. This is permissible because the song and dance sequences are conventionally coded as contracted voyeurism. (Kissing, on the other hand, belongs to the realm of the private.)

Voyeurism

Mulvey (1975) notes how through its codes and conventions, the cinema constructs the way in which women are to be looked at – scopophilia – pleasure in viewing. As holder of the gaze, the spectator is positioned voyeuristically, desiring to look, with all that that connotes in terms of fetishism. This is clearly illustrated in *Dastak* (The Knock, 1970) which achieved notoriety for a single shot lasting just a couple of seconds, in which Rehana Sultan appears in the nude. The film tells the story of a young Muslim couple Hamid and Salma, who move into an apartment in Bombay unaware that its previous tenant was a *tawaif* (an entertainer/prostitute). Her customers, not knowing that she has moved, come and knock on the door and disturb the young couple. The young people living in an apartment opposite look into the apartment and watch Salma (the young wife) as she bathes and dresses. But there is more to it. When her husband Hamid goes away to work, Salma is alone and, unaware that she is being watched by the men across the street, enacts her fantasies. 'The film hovers between the two spaces in which woman's sexuality is distributed: the home and the brothel.' In the former, woman's sexuality is reduced to its reproductive functions; in the latter, it is pure and explicit sexuality, available to all.

In the artistic cinema, directors associated with the New Cinema sought to present a very different image of women – women not as objects of male desire, but as products of diverse social formations and seeking to transcend their sordid circumstances. These directors are interested in capturing the plight of women as they are caught in the contradictory pulls of tradition and modernity, past and present, and individuality and community. Satyajit Ray's *Mahanagar* (Metropolis) is a good example. Made in 1963, it seeks to explore the influence of urbanisation on the character and behaviour patterns of a woman who, like many women in India and elsewhere, is increasingly subject to the forces of urbanisation. *Mahanagar* relates the problems and privations of Arati and her husband Subrata, who live in Calcutta. Subrata works as an accountant in a bank but his income is insufficient to meet his family obligations, so he suggests that Arati should look for employment too. At first Arati dislikes the idea but she later consents to become a salesgirl. Subrata's father, a traditionalist, is appalled by this idea, despite Subrata's attempts to convince him that times have changed. With the landing of a job, a whole new world opens up before Arati. She finds the job interesting and the people with whom she works likeable. Her boss, Mukherjee, grows to love her. Arati's father-in-law, however, steadfastly refuses to accept the money she brings home.

Arati's behaviour and outlook begin to change. The urban environment to which she is exposed is clearly having a profound impact on the way she thinks, feels and acts. She has entered the modern world. This change arouses a measure of anxiety in her husband, and through the help of an influential friend, he succeeds in securing a second job which he does after bank hours. He persuades Arati that, now that he has a second job she need no longer work. Next day, Arati goes to the office with her letter of resignation. Meanwhile, Subrata has lost his job and tries to prevent his wife from quitting hers, but events that follow leave her no option but to hand in her resignation.

In films like these we find an attempt to capture the complexities of modern life and their impact on women. Questions of rights and obligations, duties and privileges, independence and respect for authority, and other related issues influencing the life of women in India are being increasingly explored through cinema by directors associated with the New Indian Cinema.

The Representation of Women by Women Film Makers/Directors

Next, we need to examine the work of female directors, only recently emerging, and how they seek to portray the lives and experiences of women. During the last three decades a number of talented women film directors have appeared on the Indian cinema scene. Among them, Prema Karanth, Aparna Sen, Vijaya Mehta, Sai Paranjpye, Parvati Ghosh, Vijaya Nirmala, Suprabha Debi, Bhanumathi and Kalpana Lajmi deserve special mention. A few of the films made by female directors in India are now discussed in light of the themes and issues that these works explore. Almost all these directors have shown a great interest in examining the experiences, problems and hardships encountered by women, from the viewpoint of women. It has been argued by some women film critics that even the most liberal-minded and well-meaning of male film directors in India still display some residual patriarchal leanings. So it is interesting to examine how women filmmakers in India are seeking to capture cinematically the experiences of women as they explore the complex terrain of modern life.

Accordingly we have selected four women film directors – Prema Karanth, Vijaya Mehta, Aparna Sen and Kalpana Lajmi. They expose some of the tensions and contradictory pressures connected with the representation of female subjectivity in the context of the family in Indian cinema. Prema Karanth, a gifted director from Karnataka, was art director of two films, *Hamsa Geethe* (1975) and *Kudre Motte* (1977). However, the film that we wish to discuss is her *Phaniyamma* (Aunt Phani, 1982).

Phaniyamma

Based on a novel by M.K.Indira, it explores the question of female identity in an essentially male-dominated society through the life of a woman over a seventy-year period, against the background of Brahmin orthodoxy. Phani is a good-natured little girl who helps with the various household chores of the older women while her brother attends the local school. At the age of nine, as custom would have it, her horoscope is meticulously studied and compared with that of one of her equally young relatives. As the horoscopes match admirably, the elders resolve to arrange a marriage. Phani and her child husband go through the marriage ceremony, the camera beautifully catching their bewilderment and boredom. After the marriage ceremonies are over, Phani's husband goes back to his village, and she goes to live with her uncle until she reaches puberty.

Unfortunately, this carefully mapped-out scenario goes sour when Phani's little husband dies from a snake bite, and she is left a widow while still a child. Widowhood entails various humiliations and derogations. Her wedding chain (mangalsutra) is taken away; her attractive bangles are broken; the red mark on her forehead is wiped away. When she reaches puberty, her head is shaved in accordance with traditional custom. From then she is obliged to go about bald-headed, dressed in a white sari to signify her widowed state and to make herself as unattractive as possible to the opposite sex. Interestingly, as a consequence of the activities of the social reformers, the Hindu Widow's Remarriage Act and the Child Marriage Restraint Act had by then entered the statute books.

Cut off from her usual social activities, Phani endures her suffering in silence, not quite understanding the reasons for her miserable existence. As she matures, she decides to rise above the sterility of her life and invest it with meaning by helping others in society. As time passes, the unfortunate and bewildered child widow becomes the caring and compassionate Aunt Phani, a highly esteemed and much loved woman in the village who goes about helping others. She also begins to question and challenge some of the customs people have unthinkingly upheld. She helps with the complicated birth to a woman who belongs to the untouchable class. She pours scorn on the hypocrisy of a man who sleeps with an untouchable woman and ritually purifies himself the following morning. A young woman who is treated harshly by her husband for her inability to bear children is persuaded by Phani to take the extraordinarily daring step of leaving him.

Phani's growth into emotional maturity and self-confidence is vividly brought to life in one episode. Dakshyani, a sixteen year-old widow, defiantly refuses to have her head shaved as dictated by custom or to subject herself to other humiliations connected with widowhood. Her mother-in-law and other villagers are outraged by her defiance. Phani is the only person who is bold enough to side with Dakshyani; she points out that as times have changed, people need to relinquish outdated customs and obsolete ways of thinking and adopt more modern and enlightened attitudes. Dakshyani succeeds in holding her ground; she keeps her long hair and wears bright-coloured clothes. Eight months later she becomes pregnant and announces that she is planning to marry the father of the child, her brother-in-law. At the age of seventy, Phani, herself the victim of outmoded customs, has succeeded in challenging them.

Phaniyamma is a film that deals with female individuality in a male-dominated world circumscribed by immutable laws, conventions and traditions. What Prema Karanth, the director of the film, has sought to do is to call attention to the terrible plight of women in tradition-bound societies and for the need of will power, self-confidence and strength of character to overcome it. Phani, herself a symbol of submission to tradition, becomes a symbol of change as the story unfolds, and the issue of female individuality and identity is at the heart of this film.

Rao Saheb

The second film is Vijaya Mehta's *Rao Saheb* (Barrister, 1986). Mehta has a close relationship with the theatre where she distinguished herself both as a director and an actress. Her first film *Smriti Chitre* won the National Award for the best Marathi-language film of 1983. *Rao Saheb* is her second film. It explores the dualisms of tradition and modernity, inherited custom and social reform as they impinge on the lives of women. Set in the early twentieth century at a time of confrontation between Westernisation and traditional Indian culture, it explores Brahmin orthodoxy, widow remarriage and social reform – all topics that generated much discussion and debate in the 1920s. The film tells the story of a twenty-year old municipal clerk, Bhaurao and his fifteen-year old bride, Radhika. They live in a small outbuilding at the back of a mansion, which has fallen into disrepair. The mansion is owned by Rao Saheb and inhabited by three people who lead strangely isolated lives: Rao Saheb, an English-educated barrister who lives amidst an artificially created Victorian ambience, his brother, Nana Saheb, who is suffering from some mental disorder and has withdrawn into himself and Mawasi, Rao Saheb's aunt who was widowed at the age of ten and leads the austere life of a widow required by custom.

A certain gloominess, both physical and emotional, pervades the mansion and the arrival of the vivacious Radhika infuses new vitality. Mawsi takes a liking to Radhika. Radhika is fascinated by Rao Saheb and his charmingly foreign ways. It is evident that Rao Saheb is nervous and indecisive, caught as he is between two cultures. Meanwhile, Radhika gives birth to a son. Everyone in the household is overjoyed about the arrival of the baby, except the mentally deranged Nana Saheb. One night, in a heavy downpour, he leaves the house to be lost for ever. Bhaurao goes in search of him, but fails to locate him, catches pneumonia and dies soon afterwards.

Tatya, Bhaurao's father, who is given to heavy drinking, blames Rao Saheb for the death of his son and is emphatic that Radhika's hair be shaved off, as prescribed by custom. Rao Saheb, who is constantly harping on the theme of social reform, tries to dissuade Tatya, but he fails. As fate would have it, Tatya drowns in a well. At Rao Saheb's request, Radhika starts to grow her hair and wear bangles, forsakes the austere life of widowhood, and begins to educate herself. The mutual emotional attachment between Rao Saheb and Radhika seems to deepen. Mawsi tells Rao Saheb that he should marry Radhika and he accedes in principle, but cannot bring himself to act. A woman film director has here sought to capture the problems and privations of women from a feminist perspective. *Rao Saheb*, like *Phaniyamma*, touches on the themes of modernity, social change, women's identity, and the power of patriarchy.

36 Chowringhee Lane

The third film is Aparna Sen's *36 Chowringhee Lane* (1981). Aparna Sen has been associated with cinema from very early in life, first gaining critical recognition as an actress in Satyajit Ray's films, and then as a filmmaker in her own right. *36 Chowringhee Lane* is her first film and it deals with the loneliness and disappointments of an Anglo-Indian school teacher. Anglo-Indians led a precarious existence: they adopted British ways of life, wore western clothes, ate Western food, and took Christian names, but they were not considered fully British by the Indians or the British nor fully accepted by either.

One such Anglo-Indian teacher, Violet Stoneham, is the subject of *36 Chowringhee Lane* She is an ageing school teacher, trying to teach Shakespeare to an unappreciative group of girls in Calcutta. She lives on her own in a dark and dingy apartment with a cat for company. Her friends and relatives have all left India for good and all she has are memories. The only person close to her still in India is her brother Eddie who, senile and mentally deranged, is in a home for the aged.

Returning home from church on Christmas day, Violet Stoneham chances to meet Nandita, a former student. Samaresh, Nandita's boyfriend, is with her, and Violet invites them both for coffee. They accept the invitation with some reluctance because the prospect of spending some time with an old woman teacher reminiscing about her past does not particularly appeal to them. However, they quickly realise the possibilities inherent in the situation: they can use Violet's house as a place to meet in privacy rather than using taxi cabs. Samaresh persuades Violet to allow him to use her apartment while she is at school, so that he can write the novel he has long been planning to write in an atmosphere of peace and quiet.

For a while, this arrangement works well for everyone concerned. Samaresh and Nandita are able to spend time together while Violet is in school; and she in turn can return from work to an apartment full of joy and life. A warm and intimate relationship seems to develop between them. Nandita and Samaresh accompany her on walks and bring her dinner from restaurants; she plays old records for their entertainment. Violet's life is again filled with delight, and she even forgets to pay her weekly visit to her brother.

Meanwhile, the atmosphere in school is beginning to turn sour for Violet. A new head of the English department is appointed, a young Indian teacher with the right professional qualifications, but very little experience. Violet is ordered to confine her teaching to English grammar and not teach literature. As her brother becomes more feeble, he grows more irritable. However, Violet is able to face these disappointments and frustrations with equanimity because her intimate relationship with the young Indian couple gives her a much-needed sense of security and human worth. However, that too proves illusory. One day she returns to her apartment unexpectedly and finds out for what purpose the young couple has been using her apartment. Events take a turn for the worse: Eddie dies, and her last link with the Anglo-Indian world is severed. Samaresh lands a job and marries Nandita. As a wedding gift, Nandita's parents give them a fully furnished apartment. Now they have no more use of Violet's apartment. Meeting friends, attending parties and receptions, they very quickly forget Violet.

Violet finds it increasingly difficult to accept the situation. Her misery grows. She pays a visit to the young couple and expresses her hope that their relationship, which means so much to her, will once again flourish. It's Christmas once again; Violet invites Nandita and Samaresh for tea, but they decline, saying that they had made other plans and will be out of town. Violet is greatly disappointed and the film ends with Violet in total and unbearable isolation. The final image of her is on a dark and wet night, all by herself, reciting her favourite Shakespearean lines to a desolate street. Director Aparna Sen has poignantly captured the loneliness of a middle-aged woman, and she does so from within the consciousness of the lonely woman.

Parama

Aparna Sen's *Parama* (1985) also explores female identity in the context of the Indian family and the plight of women as subjects in a culture that tends to marginalise and imprison them. In *Parama*, Sen examines how the identity of women can be rearticulated in terms of the historical experience of gender. The film centres on the life of Parama as she approaches middle age; she married early and lives a sheltered life in a traditional upper-class family. She has absorbed the ethos of orthodox upper-class family living and fastidiously performs the duties expected of her as wife, mother, aunt and sister-in-law. It appears that she has managed totally to submerge her true self in the various roles assigned to her.

A family festival takes place at which Parama plays a crucial role: she is entrusted with overseeing all the details. At this festival, Parama meets the nephew of a friend of her husband's, called Rahul, who earns his living abroad as a photographer. He is visiting India and his passion for recording traditional ceremonies brings him to Parama's house for the festival. Rahul is attracted by Parama although he is much younger than she. As a friend, Rahul would customarily address her as aunt but, instead, he calls her by her first name. Parama finds this somewhat unsettling. Rahul brings to a family gathering the photographs he took at the festival, and Parama is embarrassed to find that she is at the centre of many of them. Her embarrassment grows when her nephew calls to inform her that Rahul wishes to take more photographs of her. At first Parama refuses, but later she agrees when her mother-in-law and the rest of the family convince her that it would be impolite to ignore such a request.

Rahul arrives one morning as Parama is attending to her daily household chores and photographs her. Extremely self-conscious and somewhat troubled by all this, she is relieved when Rahul leaves, saying that he has taken enough photographs. However, Rahul comes back again and asks her to introduce him to the old city. Parama's husband, Bhaskar, is away on business and so, with her mother-in-law's permission, she agrees to accompany him. Parama experiences a new sense of freedom – she finds Rahul's company invigorating. Gradually, she finds herself being emotionally drawn toward Rahul.

In accordance with family custom, Parama has always dutifully played the assigned roles of wife, mother, and daughter-in-law. Now she begins to realise that she is a woman of flesh and blood. Her married life with Bhaskar has settled into a predictable and routine round of events; she takes care of his needs, looks after their children, and maintains a comfortable home. But now she feels desire for Rahul stirring within her; his understanding of her and his pleasant ways appeal to her. Fear overtakes Parama, and she calls up her husband, who is away on business, and asks him to come back immediately. This is not the first time he has been away from home, and as everything seems to be normal, he is surprised by her request. Meanwhile, Parama resolves to be mentally strong and not see Rahul again.

But it happens that Parama meets Rahul by chance in the house of one of her friends. There she yields to her desires and delights in this new relationship; under various subterfuges she gets away from home and spends time with Rahul, A new excitement has entered her life. When Rahul leaves India again, Parama returns to her customary way of life. However, things have changed irretrievably, and neither her husband nor her household seems to have any attraction for her. Rahul writes from abroad, and Parama replies. He specifies a date for his return to India and he sends Parama a magazine featuring some of his photographs of her. On one of the photographs he has penned a message of love. Bhaskar, seeing the magazine, unsuspectingly opens it, and a storm breaks out. Parama's mother disappears to her bedroom and refuses to see her; her husband moves to another room; the children are unwillingly kept away from her; she is no longer allowed to play her earlier important role in the household. She is overcome by unbearable pain. Rahul is presumed lost or stranded in some distant country. Lacking support, Parama decides to take her life.

Parama's family finds her lying bleeding in a bath and rushes her to a nursing home. Her family, somewhat guiltily, gathers around her. She learns that Rahul has been located and is in good health. None of this seems to move Parama. The compassionate family doctor admonishes her that she should seek psychiatric counselling to recover from her trauma and erase her feelings of guilt. Parama's daughter, who had initially condemned her behaviour, now comes and sits by her.

If feminism concerns the recognition of women's predicament of oppression and marginalization because of gender, *Parama* can be described as a film with feminist vision. *Parama* in many ways departs from the standard norms of behaviour and rules of conduct advocated by most Indian films. It is hardly surprising that it generated huge controversy over matters of morality, family life and the changing mores of society.

This consideration of the works of some women filmmakers in India provides some idea of the themes and issues that they deal with. It also dispels the notion that Indian films are monolithically male-centred although the vast majority of popular films made in India do still examine the lives of women from a traditional and male viewpoint, and do portray women as objects of male desire. However, more films are being made which seek to articulate a woman's viewpoint, particularly in the New Indian Cinema.

Feminism and the New Indian Cinema

A fascinating study of the intersection of traditional Indian customs, class and caste structures with feminist issues is Kalpana Lajmi's *Rudaali* (Professional Mourner, 1992). Dimple Kapadia, a glamorous film star, plays the central role of Sanichari the bitter, lonely and hardened woman. She is a bonded labourer to the village landlord who, on his deathbed, summons a professional mourner Bhikni (Raakhee). 'The two women form a bond and Sanichari relates her story (told in flashback) of exploitation and deceit, relieved by moments of joy over her son, who has since abandoned her' (Garga, 1996). Bhikni dies suddenly of cholera but her dying message for Sanichari is that she was the mother who had abandoned her at birth. Sanichari, who has never shed a tear, cries for the first time in her life and becomes a *Rudaali,* one who cries for her living. Combining the social concerns of the 'art' cinema with elements of the mass appeal of Bombay films, *Rudaali* contains intriguing elements. For example, Sanichari is highly vulnerable to all sorts of oppressions. She resists many of them, but succumbs to the dominant discourses. Adapting Marx, one could say that as a woman she makes her own history, but not under conditions of her own choosing. There are a number of instances in the film where the essentialised notions of what it means to be a woman are invoked. When you are watching the film, what do you think of the male protagonists? How does Lajmi, the woman director, portray these?

So far we have made the contrast between popular cinema and art cinema as transparent as possible. We have seen how Indian popular films are made to a formula: concern for the family, reverence for mythological gods and goddesses and the defeat of the criminal as a result of poetic justice. Raina (1986) has drawn attention to how this formulaic narrative, supported by dreamlike visuals and interspersed with music, song and dance, projects our 'deep seated but suppressed fantasies'. The Bombay film, it is alleged, is the opium of the Indian masses. The artistic cinema, however, is to a large extent free from the excesses and the clichés of popular cinema and it 'calls into question some of our psychological and moral values and raises our consciousness about the issues it treats' (Raina 1986: 132) But the art cinema in India remains a minority art and the popular cinema can be read as some of the younger film critics have demonstrated in interesting and novel ways to yield new significances of meaning.

According to Raina (1986), there is a Middle Cinema, one that literally stands between the popular cinema and the élite art cinema. It is aimed at that section of the middle class audience 'who are satisfied with their petty-bourgeois life style and like the comforts of moderately high prosperity...' They are the products of the urban boom, they personalise politics and vote for the Congress Party out of a genuine admiration for the 'dignity and poise' of its leader' (Raina, 1986: 134). Although the Middle cinema tackles impor-tant issues, it is their treatment that differentiates this genre from both popular cinema and art cinema. Let us look at some examples.

Sai Paranjpye is a woman director who felt that the distinctions between the two types of cinema were no longer valid. Coming from a theatre and television background, her *Sparsh* (The Touch, 1979) is about Anirudth, the Principal of a school for blind children (played by Naseeruddin Shah) who is himself blind, and his clash with Kavita, (played by Shabana Azmi), a widowed teacher who works in the school. He believes that Kavita is in love with him on account of his blindness. The film is a love story and displays all the clichés of love stories in the popular cinema – 'the opening and closing songs, the stretches of visuals in which the lovers are shown in idyllic surroundings ...' The film won three National Awards and although it treats the issue of blindness without sentimentality, it does not delve deeply enough into the position of the blind (disabled) in a country like India.

Mahesh Bhatt's *Arth* (The Meaning, 1983) is about a middle class urban marriage on the verge of collapse. The husband leaves his wife to live with an artist but returns to his wife, who rejects him. This act of defiance appeals to middle class educated women who saw in the film glimmerings of protest 'against a duplicitous sexual code which condemns a woman for infractions of the marriage covenant, but condones similar lapses by men' (Raina, 1986:137). However, the 'injured' wife sets up house with her maid servant's daughter, whose mother too is maltreated by her drunken husband. The fact that the wife does not seek sexual fulfilment through another lover ensures the status quo and there is no exploration of the social and psychological factors that make for marital discord.

In *Masoom* (The Innocent, 1983), the peaceful life of a couple is 'shattered by the arrival of a small boy, the illegitimate son of the husband'. This film is a recycled version of Kramer Vs Kramer and Shekhar Kapur's (the director) handling of the theme is considered to be gentle and deft. Similar to the situation in popular films, the affair between the husband and the boy's mother is shown in flashbacks with the usual floral surroundings. However, the film side-steps the thorny issue of the status of the unwed mother in middle class society. Furthermore, as Rajadhyaksha and Willemen (1994:423) observe, the film also side-steps 'the knottier aspects of the problem by making the illegitimate child a boy and by requiring the wife to accept the fruit of her husband's infidelity rather that the other way around'.

Finally, in this Middle cinema genre, we can look at *Chakra* (The Wheel, 1980). Directed by Rabindra Dharmaraj (who died at the age of 33), it depicts life among Bombay's slumdwellers and predates Nair's *Salaam Bombay* (1988) by a few years. Amma (Smita Patil) and her son Benwa (Ranjit Choudhury) move into the squalor of a tenement in Bombay after her husband killed a money lender who tried to rape her. The husband was then shot for trying to steal some tin to build a hut. As Raina (1986:135) perceptively commented: 'the wheel of this woman's fate keeps revolving, is never steady and uproots her from not only her habitat but also her dreams'. Elements of popular cinema are again present – for example, the 'heroine's sexuality is made an object for the leering camera-eye, as in the bathing-scene'. But with such predictable cinematic strategies, this film also fails to address properly the problem of the underclass.

CHAPTER 6

Styles and Techniques

At one level, cinema is a universal art form, transcending its locality. At another level, it depends for its success on being grounded in a specific culture and drawing on its resources. Hollywood Westerns, samurai films of Japan, martial arts films of Hong Kong and the romantic musicals of India all illustrate this. This chapter focuses on the distinctiveness of Indian popular cinema.

In terms of style and techniques of presentation, Indian popular cinema is in sharp contrast to artistic films, which are generally realistic and follow the neo-realistic tradition, exploring social problems and inequities. According to Rinki Roy Bhattacharya (in personal communication), the polarisation between commercial and artistic cinema occurred in the 1960s when renowned directors such as Guru Dutt (1965), Mehboob Khan (1965) and Bimal Roy (1966) were replaced by a new breed of directors, mainly graduates of the Pune Film Institute or film society members. Notable in this emerging group (some already discussed here) and claiming parallel status were Basu Chatterjee (cartoonist in the tabloid *Blitz*), Basu Bhattacharya (assistant briefly to Bimal Roy), Mani Kaul, Kumar Sahani (graduates of Pune Institute), Shyam Benegal (from the advertisement media), Ritwik Ghatak (who scripted Bimal Roy's *Madhumati* and was a Professor of Film Direction), Adoor Gopalakrishnan (from Kerala) and Mrinal Sen (who worked as an apprentice in sound recording studio). Bhattacharya's debut film, *Teesri Kasam* (The Third Vow, 1965) was a breath of fresh air in the void left by the previous directors. A delicate love story, it won the award for best Hindi film of 1965. However, according to Rinki Roy Bhattacharya, none of his works was considered 'new wave' except *Uski Kahani* (His/Her Story, 1966). To qualify for the new wave genre ('a label thrust upon this group, indicating the European nouvelle vogue') it was obligatory for the

film to be low budget, songless and starless. These were the identification
marks, at least in the formative stage. However, Ritwik Ghatak and Mrinal
Sen, whose contributions we discuss below, are firmly located within the
new wave cinema.

Meghe Dhaka Tara

No better contrast between the commercial success of Indian popular cinema
and the box-office failures of some of the artistic films could be found than
Ritwik Ghatak's films. His films were not 'hits' and his genius has only quite
recently been acknowledged. As one commentator (Levich, 1997:30-32)
says:

> Each work is a work of genuine distinction, marked by formal daring,
> intellectual vigor, and powerful persuasion. At least two of them – The
> Cloud-Capped Star (*Meghe Dhaka Tara*, 1960) and *Subarnarekha*
> (1965) are acknowledged masterpieces whose stature has only increased
> with time.

Ghatak used melodrama in the service of high art; he made his sound tracks 'thick'; anti-naturalistic sound and eccentric focal techniques combined with his Marxist politics. But in his use of melodrama, he harked back to the Indian theatre traditions and mythical archetypes. These enabled him to satisfy his longing for his roots so as to cope with seeing his homeland, Bengal, become part of Pakistan in 1947. Hence his preoccupation with Partition and its terrible aftermath.

Mrinal Sen's influence is of a different order. His *Bhuvan Shome* (1969) –considered to be the origin of the New Indian cinema – has influenced a whole generation of filmmakers. Made on a tiny budget, *Bhuvan Shome* won the award of Best Film, Best Director and Utpal Dutt for Best Actor. Sen is generally 'regarded as the leading proponent of political cinema in India' (Vasudev, 1995:75). He is a craftsman and his experimenting with cinematic expression has earned acclaim, but time has also worked in his favour. *Bhuvan Shome* was released in 1969 when the Indian cinema was poised for change – the old order of Mehboob Khan, Bimal Roy, Guru Dutt and even Raj Kapoor was being replaced and there was a cast of almost entirely new faces – Utpal Dutt, Sushasini Mulay, Shekhar Chatterjee, Sadhu Meher and even Amitabh Bachchan to help with narration (see Mukhopadhyay 1995 chapter 4, for a comprehensive account of the film's ground-breaking nature).

Most were shot not in studios but in real locations. *Bhuvan Shome* was financed by a government agency, the FFC (Film Finance Corporation). According to Rinki Roy Bhattacharya, however, the FFC did not provide distribution for the new wave films and they were seldom granted the normal schedule of three shows per day. So even with funding, there was no distribution back-up to market the films. Sen's films, like Ghatak's, were not commercial successes. According to Mukhopadhyay (1995), Goswamy, who backed Sen's *Mahaprithivi* (Great World, 1991) later remarked: 'I would never approach an art film-walla anymore. If I make a film, I shall be out-and-out commercial'. What, then, makes Indian popular films commercially successful?

Stylisation and Popular Cinema

The popular films are mostly romantic musicals that offer escapism and fantasy worlds to the movie goers. Entertainment is their watchword. Although it is unwise to lump all popular films into a single category or to ignore their historical evolution, one can fairly identify certain characteristics in them.

In Chapter One we identified six major influences that shaped Indian popular cinema. All relate not only to content but also to the characteristic style and techniques of presentation. The first was the epics the *Ramayana* and the *Mahabharata* and their profound influence on the thought and imagination of the peoples of India and on its cinema. The art of narrative clearly owes much to the epics and particularly, to their structure. There is a circular pattern in which narratives are embedded in other narratives. Indian popular films reflect this since their narrative is rarely linear – plots branch off into sub-plots. Good examples of these narrative dispersals can be found in *Khalnayak* (1993) and *Gardish* (1993) and these two films also illustrate the changing narrative strategies of the nineties, on which we elaborate in the next chapter.

Second is the impact of classical Sanskrit theatre in Indian popular films. We have already drawn attention to its highly stylised nature and its emphasis on spectacle. In classical theatre, music, dance and gesture combine magnificently to create a vibrant artistic unit with dance and mime being central to the dramatic experience. The Sanskrit word *natya* meaning drama is derived from the root *nrit*, to dance. One can characterise Sanskrit dramas as spectacular dance-dramas and this has carried over into Indian popular films.

The influence of Sanskrit theatre was not conveyed to the cinema directly but was channelled through the regional folk-theatres of India. After the tenth century, Sanskrit theatre declined and the regional folk theatres that sprang up retained many of its stylistic elements. Through folk dramas like Yatra of Bengal, Ram Lila of Uttar Pradesh, Terukkuttu of Tamilnadu classical theatre affected popular films – the third formative influence.

The fourth was the Parsi theatre. The plays blended realism and fantasy, music and dance, narrative and spectacle, earthy dialogue and ingenuity of stage presentation, integrating them within a dramatic discourse of melodrama. The Parsi plays contained crude humour, melodious songs and music, sensationalism and dazzling stagecraft. All these elements fascinated theatre-goers who saw drama as a form of undemanding entertainment. The Parsi plays powerfully influenced Indian popular films. The styles and techniques that we associate with the popular cinema can be traced in large measure to them.

Fifthly, the impact of Hollywood is clearly discernible in Indian popular films. Its technical ingenuity appealed to Indian filmmakers, and Hollywood musicals stirred their imaginations. Hollywood musicals achieved their high point in the 1920s to the 1950s and Indian film directors were quick to draw on them for their own musicals, but with some differences in approach already discussed. For example, the Hollywood musicals had as their plot the world of entertainment itself. Indian filmmakers, while enhancing the elements of fantasy so pervasive in Indian popular films, used song and music as a natural mode of articulation in a given situation in their films. There is a strong Indian tradition of narrating mythology, history, fairy stories and so on through song and dance.

The Indian filmmakers departed from their Hollywood counterparts in another way: whereas Hollywood filmmakers strove to conceal the constructed nature of their work so that the realistic narrative was wholly dominant, Indian filmmakers made no attempt to conceal the fact that what was shown on the screen was a creation, an illusion, a fiction. However, they demonstrated how this creation intersected with people's day to day lives in complex and interesting ways.

Finally, the impact of Western musical television (MTV) is being increasingly felt in Indian films: their pace, the camera angles, the music, the dance sequences. One has only to see Mani Rathnam's *Bombay*, a popular and controversial film to realise this. These six cultural forces have shaped the style and techniques of Indian popular cinema.

A number of elements invest Indian popular cinema with a clear identity. Among these are the following:

- Indian popular films are not realistic in the strictest sense

- They seek to create a world of fantasy

- Acting is exaggerated

- All aspects of the filmic experience are melodramatic

- The use of the camera is often flashy, drawing attention to itself

- Editing is very obtrusive

- Stereotypes related to character and situation are common

- Music is central

- Songs, very often sung by well-known playback signers, are crucial in unfolding the narrative

- Dance sequences are often used to intensify the intended emotions and the spectacle

Indian popular films never pretend to be wholly realistic. The stories may be filmed in a realistic setting, but the styles of presentation are products of cultural stylisation – for instance, the way music, song and dance are deployed. Audiences are perfectly willing to accept that the hero or heroine when anxious could break into song or that they dance gaily when happy. Audiences perceive no disjuncture between the story with its realistic, everyday setting and the song and dance sequences. This is primarily because they have come to accept that films are governed by conventions commonly shared between them and the filmmakers and audiences. These conventions have evolved over time and have reached a measure of stability. Indian popular films cannot be judged by the realistic yardsticks applied to Western films. Each needs to be understood and evaluated in terms of their conventions. The style and techniques of Indian popular cinema are highly stylised.

Glamour and Overstatement

To create a world of fantasy, sets are elaborate and glittering, whether the films be religious or contemporary social dramas. The elaborate sets of the religious and mythological films are associated with royal courts or heavenly abodes. Social dramas could be set in glamorous nightclubs or upper-class mansions. One of the goals of these popular films is to provide viewers with easy routes to worlds of fantasy. The exaggeration and flashiness provide temporary satisfaction in these fantasy worlds and brief escape from the miseries and privations of daily life.

Many Indian popular films are both romantic musicals and melodramas. The fundamental trait of the melodramas is excess – the emotion is always in excess of what the situation demands and this is reinforced by both the acting style and the modes of presentation. Melodrama tends to simplify the world and present everything in stark contrasts. And this is what Indian popular cinema does.

Flashiness and exuberance characterise Indian popular cinema. Camera angles and the use of close-ups serve to call attention to the ingenuity of cameramen, quite apart from their function in advancing the story. Similarly, the editing, unlike in Hollywood films, is intentionally obtrusive although this is not to say that editors do not display any imagination or ingenuity.

Stereotypical Characterisation

Also distinctive is the representation of stereotyped characters. The heroes, heroines, villains and comedians are readily identifiable. Their demeanour, dress and gestures are highly conventionalised and immediately convey the nature of the character. It is useful to note how two comedians see their styles and techniques. Comedian Jagdeep is well-known for his role as the pick-pocket shoe-shine man in Bimal Roy's *Do Bigha Zamin* (Two Acres of Land, 1953). His style and technique, according to Rinki Roy Bhattacharya (daughter of Bimal Roy), defies fixed labels. Unlike Johnny Walker, Jagdeep's face is 'serious' and he uses every trick in the trade – facial contortions, loud guffaws, bursting into song or into tears, body language – to convey his art. Comparing the situation with what he did in the fifties, Jagdeep complains that many directors now go for cheap jokes and, worst of all, lines already written are changed overnight at the whims of a star or director.

Johnny Walker has acted in more than 300 films in a long and successful career which includes *Pyaasa* (1957), *CID* (1956), *Sahib Bibi Aur Ghulam* (Master, Mistress, Slave, 1962), *Madhumati* (1958), *Chaudhvin Ka Chand* (Full Moon, 1960), *Taxi Driver* (1954) and *Anand* (1970). His mannerisms and his comic drunken sequences are legendary, and his biggest asset is his face. He says that when people look at him, they begin laughing. In many of his films he made last-minute changes in order to maximise the humour. And he is also remembered for fronting certain memorable songs (sung by playback singer Mohammed Rafi): *Tel Maalish (Pyaasa), Ye hai bambai meri jaan (CID)* and *Jaane Kahan Mera jigar gaya ji (Mr and Mrs 55)*. Like some of the music directors, he opted out of the 1970s and early 1980s film scene because he felt that comedy had lost its charm. But he is making a come-back in the film *Stree 420* in the role of a make-up man (see *Sunday Mid-day* part 2, June 29, 1997 for a longer discussion of the return of Johnny Walker).

Music, Song and Dance Sequences

Barnouw and Krishnaswamy (1963) suggest why music and song are so popular in Indian cinema :

a) they are linked to the regional theatre of the nineteenth century, which made great use of song

b) music provides the catalyst in a country with huge linguistic diversity. Whereas regional theatres were language-based, films tended to be culture-based. Music and mythology provided common cultural bonds between the North and the South of India.

Music, song and dance have traditionally played an integral role in the daily life of Indian peoples, whether for religious and devotional purposes or for celebrations such as birthdays and weddings. So the music, song and dance sequences in the first Indian sound films were seen as natural by Indian audiences. Furthermore, since many early Hindi films were filmed staged plays, 'film music directors transplanted music and dance from the theatre to the screen.' (Arnold, 1991).

The popularity of many films depends largely on how much its music appeals to movie-goers. In the first Hindi films, as Arnold (1991) has observed, songs were used to enhance the drama rather than develop story lines. Later on, some film and music directors such as Raj Kapoor and Naushad in the 1950s, 'used film songs as an extension of the dialogue to convey story and dramatic action' (Arnold, 1991).

Music, then, fulfils a number of functions in Indian cinema. Firstly, it is a vital element of the film experience. A film is unlikely to attain mass popularity if it has no songs; indeed, long after the story of the film has been forgotten, its songs live on in the imagination of people. Secondly, songs are used for specific purposes. They help to intensify the emotions associated with a given situation; they serve to underline moral sentiments and they play an important role in generating eroticism where sexual explicitness is forbidden on screen. Indeed, it is difficult to say whether successful films owe their success to their songs or vice versa. One reason why few artistic films enjoy commercial success is because there are no songs – without them the 'average' Indian movie-goer finds films boring.

Music and songs are used as tools of narration, and there are songs for every mood and emotion – romantic, sad, devotional, patriotic, cabaret, comical or simply lullabies. But there is no compartmentalisation here – there is much crossover. Whether it be Dev Anand singing in *Guide* (1965) or *Kala Bazar* (Black Market, 1960) or Raj Kapoor in *Barsaat* (Rain 1949), devotional or sad songs are used for the romantic situations.

However, in the words of Kabir and Snell (1994:219): 'the popular music of India comes from the cinema screen, out of the mouths of the actors and actresses whose singing voices belong to invisible performers – the 'playback singers' or dubbing artists...' Playback singing dates back to the 1930s when technological developments allowed sound and picture to be recorded independently, enabling the separation of the performer on the visual film track from the singer on the sound track. Playback singing led to changes in singing styles. Singers such as K.L.Saigal, Surendra, Pahari Sanyal, Nurjehan and Suraiya were also actors and actresses; Saigal, for example, was 'untrained in classical music, yet his style of singing was in the classical mode' (Kabir, 1991).

A new style emerged when playback singers had to adapt their voices to suit the different screen characters for whom they sang. As Arnold (1991) put it:

> this technique involved not only changing vocal styles, musical styles, and pronunciation of the lyrics to match Hindu and Muslim, North Indian, South Indian, upper class and lower class screen characters, but also varying vocal range to suit old and young characters.

Some playback singers have, however, become associated not only with certain musical styles but also with specific actors/actresses. Although Lata Mangeskhar (who appears in the Guinness Book of Records as the world's most recorded artist) is extremely versatile and has sung for a variety of actresses, Mukesh's voice seems for audiences to be the voice of actor/director Raj Kapoor, who once said that 'Mukesh's voice is the voice of my soul' (Kabir and Snell, 1994:220).

Saigal's influence on singers was significant and so was the ghazal form in which he sang. The *ghazal* is a light classical Indian song form originating in Persia (Iran). The Persian *ghazal* gradually gave way to the Urdu *ghazal*, which enjoys prodigious popularity in North India and Pakistan. As Manuel (1993:90) observes: 'Although Urdu is, on the whole, a product of Indo-Muslim culture, the *ghazal* has traditionally been enjoyed and cultivated by Hindus as well.' Herein lies one of the significant contributions of Indian popular cinema to Indian society. Since linguistic diversity has been the most formidable barrier to the development of a subcontinental pop music, Indian film songs have synthesised a variety of musical elements including bhajans, qawwalis, Latin American and Western ones to create an essentially national Hindi genre. Much of the credit for this must go to talented music composers such as Naushad and S.D. Burman. According to Kabir and Snell (1994:221), in the 1950s established poets such as Shailendra and Kaifi Azmi wrote for the cinema, raising the level of the film song to a form of poetry. This national music, particularly as reflected in the 1940s, 1950s, and 1960s 'succeeded in uniting India's people where politics, economics, social class and religion have all failed' (Arnold, 1988). We pick up this success story of music in Chapter Seven.

Dance

With regard to dance, the story is rather different. Like music and songs, dance sequences are part of the formula of 'one or two stars, six songs and three dances' in every film – which still persists. But unlike music and songs, dance sequences are not always integrated into the main story.

This is due chiefly to the origins of dance itself. In Phalke's *Raja Harischandra* (1913), all the women's parts were played by men, but ultimately Phalke succeeded in persuading Kamala, a stage actress, to dance in his film *Mohini Bhasmasur* (1913). Ramchandran (1985:253) describes this dance: 'God Vishnu, incarnating as temptress Mohini, lured the demon Bhasmasur to his doom through a seductive dance'. The dancing, choreographed by Phalke himself, originated from sources that included stone carvings of temples, paintings on the walls of Ajanta caves and from Devadasi dances and 'Tamasha' (Western Indian Folk) dancing.

In its long history, dance (together with drama) was once esteemed as a sacred art. Indeed, Shiva is one of the most familiar figures of all Hindu deities as Lord of the Dance and figures of him as a male dancer, with one foot in the air, surrounded by a ring of flame, are sold in tourist shops all over India. The Devadasis – servants of the goddess – performed Bharat Natyam, a southern Indian dance form associated with the temple, while Khatak (storyteller) dance was used with music in the temples of North India as a means of conveying to the people the myths of the gods.

In the eyes of respectable society, the Devadasis were increasingly reduced to *dasis*, mere prostitutes/slaves (see Bharucha 1995 for a comprehensive account). Serious attempts were made, particularly in the 1940s, to present a complete dance film, largely as the result of Uday Sankar's efforts to rehabilitate the classical dance. *Kalpana* (Dream, 1948) crowned his efforts, but the film didn't appeal to the masses and the 'Indian cinema had failed to evolve and develop a dance-cum-musical film as a distinct genre' (Ramachandran, 1985:248).

The 1940s also saw the development of some hybrid forms of dancing which became very popular. *Jhanak Jhanak Payal Baaje* (Jangle, Jangle, Sound the Bells, 1948) had spectacular dance numbers on a variety of ancient themes. Mumtaz Ali composed most of the dances in the Bombay talkies which were singularly successful. His most famous dance spectacles were *Main Dilli Dulham Caje Re*, (*Jhoola*, 1941) *Jawanee Kee Rail Ghadi Jaye* (*Shenaz*, 1947) and *Chana Jor Gharain Babu Main Laya Majedar* (*Bandhan*, 1940). Shashi Deo, an Indian choreographer who lives in London, told us that Mumtaz Ali used simple dance steps

> ...of turning, bending and wide hand and arms gestures for his compositions. Most of this kind of dance was a chase and tease of male and female turn, similar to British music hall acts which were then very popular in British films, with sexual overtones in words and movements

Another form of dancing was popularised by Vyjayanthimala who, in the film *New Delhi* (1956), combined Bharat Nayam dance steps with Khatak dance and Bhangra, a Punjabi folk dance. What became especially popular, however, was cabaret dancing where Western, mainly Anglo-Indian, dancers like Cuckoo and Helen achieved stardom in their own right. Cabaret dancing, however, reminds us of Aruna Vasudev's comment that women are portrayed as either vamps or victims. In Indian cinema this form of dancing examplifies the objectification of woman: she is a spectacle, par excellence – a body to be looked at, the locus of sensuality, an object of desire.

Another form of dancing is used as part of the courtesan films genre. Chandra (1973) tells us that prostitution was well established and respected in ancient India. Chakravarty (1996:277) uses the terms courtesan and prostitute interchangeably and remarks that 'a complex picture emerges of an institution that was prevalent in all parts of India and toward which moral opprobrium existed side by side with widespread social acceptance'. Nonetheless, the 'courtesan films' have been instrumental in the careers of some famous actresses including Meena Kumari, Vyjayantimala, Sharmila Tagore and Rekha. *Pakeeza* (The Pure One, 1971) and *Umrao Jan* (1981) illustrate some of the significant aspects of the courtesan film. *Pakeeza*, a classic, starred Meena Kumari and was a huge box office hit. As Chakravarty (1996: 291) notes: '*Pakeeza* is poetry and fantasy and nostalgia all orchestrated together on a grand scale'. *Umrao Jan* is rated as the quintessential courtesan film of the Bombay cinema. Starring Rekha, the film 'constructs a visual and musical treat through its social tapestry, lavish sets, personalised star appeal, romantic drama, and pathos' (Chakravarty, 1996:287).

Both *Pakeeza* and *Umrao Jan* draw upon Muslim culture and here again, as in the case of music and songs, the fusion of Muslim and Hindu elements, particularly in terms of the ghazals sung by Asha Bhosle and the use of Urdu, is an important part of Hindu-Muslim unity, and so of Indian nationhood.

How Films are Made

From an Idea or a Novel to the Screen

Director and screenplay writer together discuss the characterization of the story. Next, they plot the progression: the start, middle and end. It is not necessary to remain faithful to a given novel or original story; director and writer are free to mould a story into a visual form to be translated onto film. The following stages are generally applicable to the Indian context.

Stages by which films in India are made

1   Story selected by the producer or producer/director or even an actor.

2   Screenplay writer and director together translate chosen story into cinematic form.

3   Even before final draft, the dialogue writer enters and works with director, to give it spoken expression. This helps edit out repetitions and continues to make dramatic progression.

4   Budget is discussed with executive producer. Screenplay adjusted if necessary to suit the budget.

5   Main actors and actresses are cast.

6   Financier and distributors come in once cast is known. They hear the story line. In Indian films today, they virtually dictate to the director how many songs and dances there should be in the film.

7   Entire technical unit is contracted, including music director.

8   Dates are booked for the shoot. It may take six months to three and half years to complete, depending on the stars involved and the flow of money.

9   The editor views the rushes as ready, and when it fits with other films simultaneously being edited.

10 Editor makes rough cut of all that is filmed. During gaps in shooting, the director sees rough cut, makes alterations where necessary. Financier and distributors are given screenings before they hand over further money.

11 Once film is shot, edited, viewed, discussed again and again, re-edited to suit all sorts of demands from the stars, financier and distributors, final cut is made. First married print is struck.

12 Film is shown to Board of Film Censors, which often requests changes before issuing certificate. Requisite changes made by editor in conjunction with director.

13 Music composer is shown finished film and composes music for entire film. Background is recorded.

14 Editor fits recorded background music to film, and fits in all sound effects.

15 Film is re-recorded.

16 Release print is struck.

17 Press shows are held. (Pre-release press shows and reviews are extremely important).

18 After a massive publicity campaign, the film is finally released for general release.

Source: Amit Bose (personal communication).

CHAPTER 7

Recent Developments in Indian Popular Cinema

The Winds of Change

So far, we have surveyed the Indian cinema since its beginnings in the first decade of this century until the 1960s. Some films released post-1960, have been mentioned but we have still to examine the significant developments in Indian popular cinema since the 1970s and their influence on Asian film-makers in Britain.

It is possible to identify a number of factors in the 1970s which led to a change of direction and focus in Indian cinema. Its popular genre remained firmly within the romantic/melodramatic tradition, with the usual recipe of eight or nine songs (love, devotional, folk and so on) and the same formulaic patterns that proved successful right through 1940s, 1950s and 1960s. But, in the 1970s 'a change of direction transformed the romantic song and dance extravaganza into the violent, action-packed thriller' (Arnold, 1991:220). We have commented on the period of intense political and economic instability and social dislocation in India – themes which are reflected and refracted through the films of the 1970s and 1980s. Now we look in some detail at the political, social and economic situation in India in the 1970s and 1980s.

A number of writers, Kohli (1990) among them, have commented on the period from Independence to the 1960s as one of stable, hopeful and reconstructive Nehruvian democracy. Despite the many ills and weaknesses of the nation state during the two decades following Independence, the founding fathers of India were committed to the principles of parliamentary democracy and respect for the constitution. Over the past three decades, the Nehruvian consensus built around centrist politics and the ethos of secularism and democracy has more or less disappeared (Kohli, 1990). Mrs Gandhi governed dictatorially and bypassed constitutional and legal requirements. Sharma (1994:152) records how the authors of the books he reviewed noted that:

> Nepotism, corruption and venal personal conduct became such a pervasive part of the political culture that the 'new breed of Congress politicians' engaged in an orgy of self-aggrandizement and manipulation of the political process: from using their offices to enrich family members, thwarting the democratic process by enrolling bogus members in order to produce fictitious majorities, arming gangsters and criminals and colluding with the police to capture polling-booths during elections, protecting businessmen and even Kurdish criminals from prosecution for possession of 'black money' as well as colluding with them in elaborate kick-back schemes.

Consequently, the seventies saw the emergence of cynicism on a large scale. There was an abundance of consumer goods but the majority of Indians could not afford them. 'The thought arose that nobody was going to give you what you did not grab' (Das Gupta, 1991:238).

Kothari (1988:98) describes the mood as 'less of discontent and more of dismay and growing disorientation.' She asserts that 'the decade and more since emergency has brought home to us the increasing irrelevance of mere regimes.... For some it is basically a crisis of economic performance, for others, a crisis of leadership, for still others, a crisis of character' (quoted by Kazmi, 1996:60, who adds pertinently: 'It is this crisis of character which has gradually woven its way into the cinematic discourse too.'). This was the context in which Bachchan came to fame.

New Heroes

Much has been written about Amitabh Bachchan and his dramatic rise to superstardom. Here is an actor who, according to the cultural norms of Indian cinema, was the very antithesis of the conventional Indian hero. Garga (1996:180) observes that 'At over six feet he was too tall by Indian standards, nor did he have conventional good looks'. Yet his height, his voice and his eyes came to epitomise the angry young man's quest for vengeance and justice and he mesmerised audiences in a string of films such as *Zanjeer* (Chain, 1973), *Don* (1978), *Amar Akbar Anthony* (1977), *Sholay* (1975) and *Silsila* (1981). A new recipe for entertainment emerged, combining high-pitched melodrama, sex and violence. *Sholay* (1975) is a good example of the genre which prevailed during the 1970s and 1980s.

Basically, *Sholay* is the story of revenge wreaked by a retired police officer Thakur Saheb (Sanjeev Kumar) who hires two prisoners, Veeru (Dharmendra) and Jaidev (Bachchan) to hunt down a gang of bandits led by Gabbar Singh (Amjad Khan). Dissanayake and Sahai (1992:54) relate that:

> Some time in the past, the Thakur, then a young police officer, had arrested Gabbar Singh. However, the thug had succeeded in escaping from prison, and avenged himself by brutally killing the Thakur's family, and cutting off his arms. How the hired gunmen fight Gabbar Singh and the violence that ensues, form the bulk of the story.

Many commentators have praised the technical accomplishment of the film. It has all the trappings of a western: rugged countryside, bandits on horseback, fierce gun fights and even a gangster's moll. But here the analogy ends. For *Sholay*, according to Garga (1996:184) made violence a highly marketable commodity: 'Bachchan was no longer the avenger seeking justice but a mercenary selling his prowess as a killer, for a price.' Furthermore, in *Sholay* evil is gratuitous, pervasive and inescapable; thus it differs from earlier films such as *Kismet* (Fate, 1943) and *Awaara* (1951), where evil too is present. In *Sholay* Gabbar Singh, the archvillain, turned out to be the most popular of all the characters, according to an analysis of audience reception of the film by Dissanayake and Sahai (1992). Sholay ran for five consecutive years in Bombay and became a legend.

This new entertainment formula prevailed throughout the 1970s and 1980s. It had a number of consequences on the film industry. Bachchan himself, who has become a cult figure, is the son of a famous Hindi poet and one of the intellectual and social élite, a childhood friend of Rajiv Gandhi. When Bachchan seriously injured himself in a stunt in 1982 while filming *Coolie* (1983), the Indian world practically came to a standstill. Millions of people in India and abroad prayed for his recovery. Here was a member of the Indian élite who identified himself with the oppressed, became a rebel and a model of hope in a ruthless, unfeeling world. The links with the political and social aspects of India in the 1970s are clear. *Sholay* presents a feudal society consisting mostly of peasants serving a Zamindar-like aristocrat. Mrs Gandhi's imposition of a State of Emergency in 1975, at the time *Sholay* was released, was a last ditch effort to prop up a government which had lost control over urban crime, spiralling inflation, corrupt and sectarian politics and moral standards (see Garga, 1996).

Another shift in the films which had Bachchan in the leading role was the diminishing importance of music and songs. There were only three or four per film and for the first time they were extrinsic to the narrative. Furthermore, Bachchan himself (not reckoned to be a good singer) sang a number of songs in the folk idiom, which really does not require great musical ability. For example, he sang a North of India folk song *Mere Angane me tumhara kya kam hai?* (Why are you here in my backyard?) which is commonly associated with *hijras* (eunuchs), while dressed as a woman. 'The song itself was vulgar, suggesting that husbands with large wives should not despair because, of course, they would not need pillows in the bed' (Mishra *et al.,* 1989:60).

Thus, the 1970s and 1980s saw the decline of the romantic hero and heroine as incarnated by Raj Kapoor, Rajesh Khanna, Nargis and Waheeda Rehman and so on. According to Das Gupta (1991:238): 'the seventies no longer adored women, but asserted openly the right to treat them as chattels. In many parts of the country, women were molested, raped and burnt for dowry with greater impunity than ever before...' This theme brings us to Indian popular cinema in the 1990s.

New Heroines

With the arrival of the angry young man – the anti-hero – in the 1970s, the role of the heroine also changed. At first she plays second fiddle to the hero. Rao (1989) argues that 'she is ill-treated by society, seduced, raped and widowed in violent action' – all to build up the macho image of the hero. A number of films were built around this new situation. Until the late 1970s explicit rape as the central theme of a film was unusual. Indian films often featured attempted rape – one of the earliest was in *Swayam Siddha* (1948), where a wife caring for her mentally retarded husband is lusted after by her father-in-law. In one scene she pours boiling oil on her father-in-law when he tries to corner her in the kitchen. In *Mother India* (1957) too, there is attempted rape. But it is B.R.Chopra's *Insaaf Ka Tarazu* (The Scales of Justice, 1980) which is generally regarded as the first 'rape movie'. Much attention has focused on Zeenat Aman, a former beauty queen playing the lead role and it is alleged that the commercial success of the film was due to scenes of the rape of her and her sister, Padimini Kohlapure, staged with voyeuristic relish. The film attracted considerable controversy.

Typically, the success of *Insaaf Ka Tarazu* precipitated a spate of films dwelling on rape and vengeance, cashing in on a successful formula. *Pratighat* (Retribution, 1987) revolves around 'corrupt politicians and the ongoing crisis over law and order in a small town' (Gopalan, 1997:47). However, the main theme is the humiliation of a college teacher, Lakshmi. An ordinary housewife, she is disrobed by the villain, Kali, on the street in front of her house, with her family and the neighbours watching in silence. 'She walks out on her cowardly husband and aborts the child she has been carrying, not because she wants to assert her right over her body but to free herself for action' (Rao, 1995: 250). She joins forces with Durga, who had been gang raped by Kali and finally hacked him to death.

In *Zakmi Aurat* (Injured Woman, 1988) a policewoman, played by Dimple Kapadia, is subjected to multiple rapes. When the judiciary refuses to convict the rapists, the policewoman joins forces with rape victims in the city and they plan to trap the rapists and castrate them in revenge.

These three films belong to what Mathili Rao (1988) has called 'the lady avengers'. They have some common features: in *Insaaf Ka Tarazu* and *Zakmi Aurat*, the leading roles are played by well-known beautiful actresses – Zeenat Aman and Dimple Kapadia; in *Pratighat*, a beautiful newcomer, Jayata Metha plays the lead. The serious shortcomings of the law are emphasised in all three and the framing of the narrative has undertones and explicit references to the nation state and to the *Ramayana* and the *Mahabharata*. Thus, in *Insaaf Ka Tarazu*, the female protagonist is Bharati – the feminine name in Hindi for India; in *Pratighat*, she is Lakshmi (goddess of wealth) and the villain is Kali (the avenging goddess), and *Zakmi Aurat* features photographs of Gandhi on the courtroom walls and footage of the Indian flag. Even the disrobing of Lakshmi in *Pratighat* is a reminder of the disrobing of Draupadi, the wife of the Pandavas, in the court of Hastinapur.

But the most important point is that the climate of the 1980s allowed such films not only to be released but also to be box office hits. Conditions provided fertile ground for the making and the success of such films. About *Insaaf Ka Tarazu*, Rajadhyaksha and Willemen (1994:416) remark:

> This notorious rape movie followed in the wake of growing feminist activism in the 1970s after the Mathura and Mayu Tyagi rape cases, the amendment to the Rape Law and the impact of e.g. the Forum Against Rape, which offered legal assistance to rape victims.

It was probably the Mathura case which provided the catalyst for the campaign against rape and made it a public issue. Mathura, a very young girl, was raped by policemen within the precincts of a rural police station in Maharashtra. In *Whose News?* Joseph and Sharma (1994, chapter 5) refer to the sexist judgement of the court and provide a comprehensive account of the campaign against rape and the relationship between certain newspapers and the campaign. National protest about the Mathura case led to amendment of the law relating to rape.

Bandit Queen

This new trend generated a number of films, some of them originally banned by the censor and requiring several deletions before being allowed for general release – for example, Chopra's *Aaj Ki Aurat* (Today's Woman, 1993). But the film which marked a turning point in this genre is *Bandit Queen* (1995). It is based on what its director, Shekhar Kapur, calls the 'true story' of Phoolan Devi, a low caste woman. Married at the age of 11 to a much older man who rapes her, she runs away, gets into trouble and is locked up by the police, who gang rape her. Once out of jail she joins a gang of bandits and becomes the most celebrated bandit in Northern India's Chambal Valley. Through her activities, issues of caste, class and gender warfare in rural India are played out to such an extent that the military is sent in to ensure her surrender. (See Danda, 1997 for a semiotic approach to *Bandit Queen*.)

The film received rave reviews, particularly outside India. Shyam Benegal said that it is possibly the greatest film ever made in India. Its impact on the Indian film industry is significant. Pendakur (1996) has documented some of its implications for the government and for the film industry. In his view, some of the problems associated with the film are due to Phoolan Devi's initial opposition to its release; consequently, the Delhi High Court banned the public exhibition of the film on account of the dispute between the producer and Phoolan Devi. Eventually, she made a deal with Channel 4 in England and a few cuts were made to get the film through the Censor Board in Bombay. Pendakhur (1996:162) asserts that 'censorship is inherently coercive and that it limits artistic and political expression in Indian cinema.'

While Phoolan Devi was set free by the Supreme Court in 1994 after the criminal cases against her were dropped in the public interest – she is now a Member of Parliament for Mizapur – another woman, Kiran Bedi has also 'made news'. She joined the police force – a male bastion – intent on shaking it up and became the inspiration for a number of 'uniformed heroines' both on TV (in the series *Uddan*) and in the film *Tejaswini*. This remake of the highly successful Telugu film *Karthavyam* (1983) has interesting implications for the role of women in India. Inspired by the exploits of a woman police officer, Kiran Bedi, *Tejaswini* tells the story of a small-town girl who refuses to do the domestic chores. Instead, she is the super-cop who fights injustice, oppression and crime, 'despite the pressures from family, her superiors and the Mafia. In fact, she refuses to give in even when the bad group reduce her into a physical wreck' (Kazmi 1996:108). The film of her story and actions has stimulated girls in Andhra Pradesh to join the police.

Vengeance and Villiany

In addition to this theme of 'lady avengers' there is explicit violence and vengeance by male stars in a number of films released during the 1980s and 1990s. We have already seen it in Amitabh Bachchan's films – taking the law into one's own hands. A number of male stars vied to take over from Amitabh Bachchan as the top star when his films started to falter at the box office, among them Sanjay Dutt, Anil Kapoor and Jackie Shroff. Initially, Sanjay Dutt looked the most likely, but his spell in jail for alleged terrorism spoilt his chances. *Khalnayak* (1993) was highly successful and it turned out to be prophetic: Sanjay Dutt played Balu, a terrorist bent on destabilising India, although the film was made many months before his arrest. *Khalnayak* tells 'the story of a violent gun-toting terrorist, Balu, who works for a villainous 'foreign' boss who masterminds attacks on the political stability of India from abroad (implied Pakistan/Dubai).' There is a link with films like *Roja* (1992) and *Bombay* (1994), both already discussed. They reflect the unease, tensions and conflicts generated by fears of terrorism and the rise of Hindu fundamentalism and it is symbolic that *Khalnayak* begins and ends on frames of the Indian flag.

Readers are already aware of the circular style of narrative common in Indian popular cinema A new narrative strategy has developed in the 1990s and it is described by Doraiswamy (1994) In the 1990s the era of the persona has ended, the last one being Amitabh Bachchan. Heroes, heroines and villains now display the ability, in Doraiswamy's words, 'to contain within themselves more than one – if not many – stereotypic selves'. Shah Rukh Khan in *Baazigar* (Loser Takes All, 1993) and *Darr* (Fear, 1993) exemplifies the villanous hero 'and the villain in many films today also carries the onus of providing comic relief in the narrative: Anupam Kher and Kader Khan, followed by Shakti Kapoor, are the new villain-comedians'. And the heroine has taken on several functions of the vamp of yesteryear: Karishma Kapoor, for instance, in her dance sequences in *Raja Babu* (1994) and *Khuddar* (His Own Man, 1994) 'outdoes any cavorting that the Helens and the Bindus indulged in earlier in the explicitness of the sexually suggestive poses that are simulated.' (Doraiswamy 1994:4).

Villainy itself has changed. While an actor like Amrish Puri can still rely on his alarming physical appearance to convey a villainous presence, villainy is newly interpreted:

> Villainy used to be associated with vice – a moral category. The villains were bosses of dens of vice – 'bad' characters and vamps hung around drinking, gambling, smoking... Today's villains inhabit indigenous body-

building gyms (akhadas), homes realistically set up, or just walk in and out of spaces that the protagonists move in (Doraiswamy, 1994:8).

Another common strategy of old is the flashback. This has 'traditionally served to recall, to highlight, to fit in pieces of a puzzle, to justify an action currently being carried out'. This device is extended in films, such as *Tezaab* (Acid, 1989) and *Khalnayak* (The Villain, 1993). In *Khalnayak*, for example, mother and son develop the notion of 'objectivity' by recounting, separately, to two different listeners, how the villainous Roshibaba came into their lives, leading to the breakup of the family and the son becoming the villain's chief aide.

Khalnayak also became notorious for the song *Choli Ke peechhe Kya hai?* (What's behind your blouse?) which 'became the song of 1993 and was banned on Doordashan and All India Radio for obscenity' (Thomas, 1995). Although, as we have seen, the number of songs in each film declined in the 1970s and early 1980s, music, song and dance returned to the screen with a vengeance by the late 1980s. The annual 1989 international edition of *Stardust* film magazine commented thus about four recent film hits:

> In fact, there is a realisation that it is the music that has made these films a great success. There is a music madness that is raging in the industry. Every film maker is trying to cash in on this trend ... Without a doubt it is music that holds sway today.' (Cited by Arnold, 1991:221)

The return of music and songs to the film industry is interesting. *Hum Aapke Kain Houn* (*HAKH*, 1994), discussed earlier, brought back the magic touch of music with fourteen songs. From 1993 to 1994 film songs like *Didi tera devar delwana* (HAKH), *Mast Mast* (*MOHRA*), *Jaadu teri nazar* (*DARR*), *Chura Ke dil mera* (*Main Khilali Tu Anari*), *Ek Ladki Ko dekha* (*1942: A love story*), *Yeh Kali Kali Aankher* (*Baazigar*), *Ole Ole* (*Yeh Dillagi*), *Ruk Ruk* (*Viyaypath*) blared from radios, cars, buses, restaurants, discos. It is reminiscent of the popularity of music and songs in the 1950s and 1960s but now television too is in on the act.

While music directors such as Anil Biswas and Salil Chaudhury had left the film industry because they felt that trends of the 1970s and early 1980s stifled their creativity, a younger generation joined the music industry. A.R.Rahman, Bappi Lahiri and Anu Malik are among the most successful. Commenting on the music mania which invaded the film industry in 1993 and 1994, Chandra (1994) reports that Anu Malik had 35 films in hand and that the lyricist Sameer was working on 100 films at once. Since the odds of hitting the jackpot in music are very slim – the Hindi film industry allegedly works on the 20:80 hit to flop ratio – the larger music companies can, according to Chandra (1994), 'recover investments on flop film music by selling it in combination with the hits'.

However, things are changing in the music world due largely to satellite TV. Indian music is on a par with music from all over the world. Consequently, anything can become a hit and the variety of hits is staggering: for example *Mast Mast* is synthesised qawwali, *Ruk Ruk* is Indianised rap and *Choli Ke Peechhe Kya* is folk music.

Increasingly, music is creating a market for a film before its release, providing a 'hook' for the audience. Chandra (1994) quotes Shah Rukh Khan as saying: 'Music is the ad campaign for the film', and songs such as *Ruk Ruk* or *Mast Mast* are promoted on film posters. The music can compensate for a mediocre film: *Mast Mast* has boosted the film *Mohra*, reckoned to be of 'average' quality. Furthermore, a hit song can boost the standing of film stars. Madhuri Dixit came into the limelight with *Ek, Do, Teen*; Raveena Tandon is the *Mast Mast* girl and Shilpa Shetty's *Chura Ke dil Mera* has worked wonders for her.

Cinema and Television

Television is an important medium for popularising music and songs, but has only recently become part of the lives of Indians. Television began in the 1950s, as an educational medium (a pilot Unesco-sponsored educational project started in September 1959), 'broadcasting instructional fare for schoolchildren and farmers in and around Delhi' (Mitra, 1994). The Asian Games held in New Delhi in 1982 promoted television as a popular medium and since then, Doordashan, the television system in India, has played an increasingly important role in Indian culture. How has it affected the film industry?

The first indigenous soap was *Hum Log* (We People) and by the early 1980s there were a number of social soap operas such as *Buniyaad* and detective serials such as *Kohl*. Film producers (such as Chopra) soon saw the potential of television and joined the bandwagon, introducing serials based on famous Indian mythological epics. This harks back to the beginnings of Indian cinema and Phalke's *Raja Harischandra* (1913). Starting with the *Ramayana*, Doordashan capitalised on its success and serialised the *Mahabharata* from 1988-1990, which became the most popular serial of the time.

The growing popularity of the video recorder and the flourishing of video piracy – it is estimated that 95% of video cassettes in circulation in India are pirated – rendered the small screen increasingly important. Singh (1989) reports that in the 1980s, the Bombay film industry became increasingly involved in Doordashan, 'with actors, producers and directors participating in TV programming, making Indian television more filmic'. The style of Indian popular cinema is replicated in the serial *Mahabharata*, for instance in the weddings of Arjuna and Subhadra and of Abbhimanyu and Uttara. In Singh's words: 'Subhadra is portrayed coyly awaiting Arjuna on her bridal bed, with flashbacks of singing and dancing in the rain, and the camera gently sweeps closely over her body while circumnavigating the bed' (p.85). Draupadi's near rape by Keechak is portrayed in the style of the Indian cinema and the interpretation of motherhood also follows the cinema's style. As Singh (1989) says: 'Motherhood figures in an hysterical, predominantly weepy role, all kinds of mothers, happy or sorry. Kunti, Devki, Gandhari cry either out of joy or sorrow over sons, another Bombay 'filmic' trait.' (p.87).

Some commentators, Ray and Jacka (1996) among them, have argued that Doordashan, as a government monopoly, tended to produce and circulate a 'Hindu-Hindi' image of Indian national identity. In the 1980s came cable, satellite and new private services, and the breakdown of Doordashan's monopoly.

In an analysis of the audience for Indian television, Ray and Jacka (1996:84) say that

> from the point of view of the disparaties of wealth, there are three distinct audiences in India: the educated urban elite; the semi-urban market – both of these audiences are fluent in English – and the rural uneducated population.

Given that high quality programming is expensive and requires a good supply of skilled professionals, a substantial number of programmes are film-based, featuring 'film songs, stars and feature films'. This has created a boom for the record companies' revenues and 'the film industry's main earnings now come from its sale of music'. As Ray and Jacka (1996:93) relate:

> Doordashan formerly charged producers of new and forthcoming films a fee for showing songs and clippings of these films. Now the system has reversed, with D.D (Doordashan) having to pay the producers – this indicates the popularity of these programmes as well as D.D's lost monopoly.

Indian Cinema Beyond National Borders

Indian cinema has had significant impact on diasporic Asians and particularly on Asian films made in Britain. The arrival of cable and satellite in India has led to 'the great television scramble.' An important consequence of this liberalisation is the establishment of foreign-owned and Indian-owned private networks to compete with Doordashan. In this respect, Zee TV, an Indian-owned network, for example, has become the most popular satellite channel and is well established in Britain. Likewise, the export of videotapes has increased substantially, both in terms of revenue and in reaching new territories, as Pendakur and Subramanyam (1996:77) show in the following table.

Export of Videotapes to selected countries (sales shown in rupees)

Country	1987-88	1991-92
Australia	–	479,594
Bahrain	5,359	272,905
Canada	469,782	2,119,192
France	–	25,850
Germany (West)	31,163	9,397
Hong Kong	927,767	11,791,130
Kenya	–	1,245,079
Malaysia	381,197	2,578,352
Mauritius	295,224	948,921
Nigeria	–	3,978,571
Singapore	369,208	15,276,088
United Arab Emirates	4,515,795	10,334,904
UK	8,095,948	35,878,926
USA	915,006	4,990,632
USSR	4,585,000	128,431

Source: Reserve Bank of India

The availability of Zee TV on satellite and cable network and the popularity of Sunrise Radio in Britain are features of the changing Asian landscape. So is the rise of Asian filmmakers in Britain.

Earlier on, we mentioned briefly the contributions of Gurinder Chadha, Mira Nair and of Hanif Kureishi, the screenwriter of *My Beautiful Laundrette* (1984), one of Channel Four's international successes. His work documents the lives of marginalised young people, immigrants from former British Colonies, leftist intellectuals, gays, lesbians, homosexuals and 'those individuals who cross class, ethnic and sexual boundaries'. *My Beautiful Laundrette* focuses on Omar, a Pakistani caught between two worlds:

> Those of his leftist intellectual father and of his uncle Nasser, a wealthy slumlord who lets his nephew revamp one of his laundromats. Omar first employs and then becomes lovers and partners with a former school chum Johnny (Newcomb, 1997:914).

Kureishi has also written the screenplays for *Sammie and Rosie Get Laid* (1987), *London Kills Me* (1991) and *The Buddha of Suburbia* (1993).

Parminder Dhillon-Kashyap (1988) describes how the nostalgic tales of the Raj made by the British heighten colonial images and do not really challenge the morality of imperialism. Over the past decade, at least two Asian filmmakers have made their mark on the British cinematic scene: Gurinder Chadha and Mira Nair.

Gurinder Chadha was born in Kenya but has lived in Britain most of her life. After graduating at the University of East Anglia, she went into radio journalism and joined the BBC in 1988. She has produced a number of films starting with *I'm British But...*, in which she explored issues of identity among a group of British-born Asians in the late 1980s. She has made a number of documentaries for television and her *Acting Our Age* (1992) 'featured Asian Londoners, all aged over sixty, shooting and editing their experiences of ageing in Britain' (Bhattacharya and Gabriel, 1994).

Bhaji on the Beach (1993) was made by Umbi Films for Film Four International (backed by Channel Four). It features a day's outing for a group of Asian women of various ages, organised by the Saheli Women's Centre. Marketed as a seaside comedy, the film combines a number of genres, mixing irony with comedy, as it follows the women from Birmingham on their day-trip to Blackpool. It is in a sense a 'road movie' and is within the category of women's films, since women's experiences are its central theme. Using 'a range of seemingly very English iconography – including a version of the 1950s song 'Summer Holiday' sung in Punjabi as part of the sound track, the film explores the theme of what is central in living in Britain and, as the characters reveal, it is not being western or being Asian but being both' (Bhattacharya and Gabriel, 1994).

Nair has three feature films to her credit. The latest, *Kama Sutra – A Tale of Love* (1997), has provoked much controversy, particularly in India. Her first feature film, *Salaam Bombay* (1988) won the Camera d'Or in Cannes in 1988 and was nominated for the Academy Award (Oscar) for the Best Foreign Film. *Salaam Bombay* offers a sociological study of Bombay's underworld, its abandoned children, the exploitation of prostitutes and their powerlessness to hit back. Film critic Sridhar (1989) summed it up thus:

> Like the trains that have no home and flit from station to station, the children and adults of Bombay are constantly on the move seeking something elusive – a family, money, the village, happiness, death.

In *Mississippi Masala* (1991), Nair tackles another sort of problem – ignorance and misconceptions as the bases of prejudice against other communities. The film tells the story of an Indian family caught up in Idi Amin's expulsion of Asians from Uganda, who emigrate to Greenwood, Mississippi in the USA. The daughter, Mina (played by Sarita Choudhury) falls in love with Demetrius (Denzel Washington) an African-American, and their relationship becomes sexual. The Indian family is traumatised by this and the film depicts the cultural boundaries – Indian and African-American – that Mina crosses and the enormous problems caused by Mina's social mobility. Issues such as internalized racism within the Indian community and the racial animosities between Indians and blacks are made transparent. One of the strengths of the film is its featuring of Indians, Africans and African-Americans as central characters. In an interview some years after the film's release Nair said:

> If I were to find a common thread in my work, I would have to admit that I have always been drawn to stories of people who live on the margins of society – on the edge, or outside, learning the language of being in-between, always dealing with the question : what, and where, is home? These concerns are, of course, inextricably linked with my personal history as well, since I have spent most of the past years living between two worlds. (quoted by Negi, 1994-5)

What and where is home are powerful and disturbing questions and these lie at the heart of some films by Asian filmmakers working abroad. For example, in 1992 Srinivas Krishna directed *Masala*, a feature film set within the community of Indian immigrants in contemporary Toronto, which sets out to use and 'satirise elements of the Bombay Cinema to comment critically on Western multiculturalism as well as on the Indian community's own problematic identity politics.' The film explores the experiences and feelings of the young rebel Krishna who 'is equally alienated by the culture and traditions of his motherland, by the way his own family and community try to hold on to those traditions, and by the larger, still racist, Canadian society' (Interview – Srinivas Krishna talking to Roy Grundman, 1994).

In Nair's latest film, *Kama Sutra – a Tale of Love*, her objective is to be an iconoclast. Nair believes that the *Kama Sutra* is severely misunderstood both in India and in the west and she asserts that her film has much more to do with sexual politics than with sexual positions – it is not simply a sex manual but about how to handle love – 'the philosophical, the spiritual and the skill aspect, too. Kama and Sutra mean lessons of love and my film is about the many faces of love from a time (the 16th century (when sexuality was not taboo.' (quoted in HOT TICKETS, *Evening Standard*, 19 June 1997:12). But there is at least one thread which links *Kama Sutra – A Tale of Love* with Nair's earlier films: the story is about women who, 'in the course of navigating this territory of existing for men's pleasure, actually empower themselves and each other.'

Music among British Asians

Indian popular cinema, particularly through the influence of its music, is producing a different kind of empowerment – its impact on the reconfiguration of diasporic Asians is powerful. Let us look at the situation in Britain.

The involvement of the Muslim communities in Britain in Indian popular cinema is increasingly evident but Pakistan is producing more films and their international stars now feature on Zee TV in Britain. The role of music in the Muslim communities in Britain is particularly intriguing, as Baily's (1995) research on the role of music in certain British Muslim communities reveals. Although the majority of British Muslims come from South Asia, there are considerable differences among them. Baily (1995:77) identifies three main groups: the Mirpus from Azad Kashmir in Pakistan, Khalifas from Gujarat in India and Afghans chiefly from Kabul.

Only the Mirpus appear to be indifferent to music; although they enjoy it in the Hindi and Urdu movies which, according to Baily (1995), they watch on their home videos or hear on Sunrise Radio. The Khalifas are substantially involved in music, particularly Indian popular music.

> Several of the most prominent Asian professional musicians living in London are Khalifas, often seen as accompanists on BBC Asian music television programmes. Naya Saz, Sargam, Khilona Arts and Diwana Arts are examples of predominantly Khalifa bands in Britain. They play a highly amplified vision of film *git* ... (Baily, 1995:82).

Afghans are also heavily involved in music, the kind that prevails in Indian popular cinema. Kabul's radio and TV station have been destroyed and Afghan musicians in Britain are intent on re-creating their music of some 25 years ago. Baily (1995) reports that the Society of Afghan Residents in the UK has organised concerts of Afghan music with visiting Afghan artists such as woman singer Ustad Mahevash. To some extent Afghan music in Britain seems to have been inspired 'by the popularity of bhangra music among other South Asian communities in Britain' (Baily, 1995).

Bhangra Music among British Asians

Bhangra music is a highly significant musical force among Asians in Britain. Bhangra, originally a male form of rural folk music and dance from the North Western state of Punjab, was brought to Britain by Punjabi immigrants in the 1950s and 1960s. It celebrates *baisakhi* (the Punjabi new year) and the bringing in of the harvest.

> In keeping with the character of the people, it is vibrant, rhythmic and joyfully hedonistic and the language in which it is sung has been described as the 'cockney of India' (Banerji, 1988).

Bhangra musicians perform at religious and social functions all over Britain. The first generation of Bhangra musicians probably used the music to develop a sense of Asianness in the midst of the racism they faced. Channi, the lead singer of Alaap, the first group to popularise bhangra in South Asian British communities in the late 1970s, says:

> We noticed that young Punjabis in London knew little about their own culture and language and were immersed in the English disco scene. We started our bhangra songs to bring them back into their own culture. But for the music to appeal to them, we had to add the western touch with a drum beat and synthesisers. (quoted by Gopinath, 1995:309)

Since the 1980s bhangra music has drawn upon other forms of music such as reggae, house and soul. Two of the best known singers are Apache Indian and Sagoo. Apache Indian uses reggae and Jamaican patois and Sagoo mixes traditional Sufi devotional songs with rap and reggae and both of them have achieved international fame.

Qawwali

The popularisation of this musical form of the Sufi mystic tradition is due mainly to Nusrat Fateh Ali Khan, whose death in August 1997 at the age of 48 has robbed the world of qawwali's foremost exponent. His main achievement was to create a new kind of music by using Western musical instruments and by fusing the traditional with the modern.

Qawwali is a derivative of the world *qol* – the saying; it is rhythm-oriented and has a distinctive style. What Nusrat did was to increase the tempo and improvise by repeating phrases often in complex rhythmic patterns to produce an ecstatic, trance-like effect. Although he was criticised by fundamentalist critics in Pakistan, he was attracted to the East-West fusion and his voice was used in Gabriel's soundtrack for *The Last Temptation* (1988) and a string of albums for Gabriel's label, including *Shahbaaz* (1991) and *The Last Prophet* (1994). He also composed the score for *Bandit Queen* (1995).

Documentary Films – Cinema of Resistance?

Nair started her filmmaking career by making documentaries. Independent documentary film production in Britain has a long history, but in India it was until recently a virtual monopoly of the government. Understanding its purposes both here and in India illuminates an aspect of Indian filmography often ignored in studies of Indian cinema.

Nair's *Far from India* (1982) is a documentary about an immigrant newspaper seller working in New York's subway, and his estrangement from his wife when he returns home to see his new-born son. But it was her documentary *India Cabaret* (1985) which brought her into the limelight. This documents 'the double standards that the typical Indian middle-class man indulges in as he constantly distinguishes between the 'bad woman' for whom he is a customer and the 'good woman', his wife' (Negi, 1994-5:26). Controversial as this documentary was, it won Nair the prize for Best Documentary at the American Film Festival and the Global Village Film Festival. In 1986/7 she produced *Children of the Desired Sex*, a documentary about 'amniocentesis and the manner in which it is abused to abort unwanted female foetuses' (Negi, 1994/5:26).

Commentators (Chatterjee, 1994; Pendakur, 1995 *inter alia*) have noted that independent documentary film production in India is of recent origins. Although the Film Division was established as far back as 1948 to serve the informational and propaganda needs of various ministries of the Central Government and offered some funds to freelancers, the amounts were rather limited. The situation has improved substantially over the last twenty years, particularly after the 'National Emergency' of 1975, when all the civil and individual liberties guaranteed in the Constitution were withdrawn. Funds can now be raised through Doordashan and foreign television channels. Pendakur (1995:1) mentions the short film *Waves of Revolution* (1976) made by a young student, Anand Patwardhan, which captured some of the massive student protests and the popular resistance that preceded the Emergency.

Anand Patwardhan has since become famous for his documentary films which explore issues of civil rights, secularism and the unjust ways of the existing system and which are illustrative of what Pendakur (1995) calls the Cinema of Resistance. Patwardhan's interest is to get the communities involved in the issues he is dealing with. *We Make History* (1993) and *Bombay Our City* (1985) each captures performances that were put on by this community. *Raam Ke Naam* (In the Name of God, 1992), is about the resurgence of Hindu fundamentalism and exposes the forces that play havoc in the name of religion. In this as well as in his *Father, Son and Holy War* (1993) Patwardhan uses film to record and dissect social and political conflict in India. Pendakur (1995) has shown how music and song 'play important roles in the story telling in the documentary mode'. *We Make History* and *Bombay Our City* feature street plays with plenty of music and dance, while in *Raam Ke Naam*, background songs locate a set of values that are 'meant to draw viewers' attention to an earlier period in Indian history when harmonious relations existed between Hindus and Muslims' (Pendakur, 1995:2).

Well-known directors such as Kumar Shahani and Mani Kaul have also made documentaries. Mani Kaul has produced a string of documentaries such as *Yatrik* (The Traveller, 1966), *Arrival* (1980), *Before my Eyes* (1988) and *The Cloud Door* (1994). Riyad Vinci Wadia recently produced *Fearless! The Hunterwali Story* as a warm tribute to his great-aunt Mary Evans, who became Nadia, the much-loved queen of the Hindi action films from the late thirties to the early fifties. It is likely that documentary film production will soon achieve higher status, to judge by the success of the first Bombay International Film Festival of Shorts and Documentaries (BIFFSD), held in March 1990. According to Rinki Roy Bhattacharya (1990), the festival director felt that its impact was 'to break mind blocks about documentaries' and said:

> Somehow, in the film world, what with all the glamour of box office hits, stars and superstars, the documentary films have been treated as an appendage of the feature film, the theatrical hit. Through this very first Bombay International Film Festival, we hoped to reiterate the vital

importance of such films, and also celebrate the brilliance and commitment of their makers.

Attempts by some women writers to address female powerlessness can also be in the form of documentaries. For example, Rinki Roy Bhattacharya's *Char Diwari* (Behind Closed Doors, 1990) is 'a survival saga of four women, from four social backgrounds with a common bond – all four are victims of wife abuse'. In contrast to the images of motherhood depicted in the popular films, Bhattacharya's *Janani* (Mothers, 1995) is autobiographical. In it, Bhattacharya confronts her dual role of woman and mother – particularly the gap left by her three children, now adults. The crucial question for her is: 'Since my children, now adults, could survive with me or without me, could I do without them?' The film is a nostalgic celebration of mothers, grandmothers, relatives and all children, born and unborn.

Some age-old issues are also acquiring increasing importance. For example, *Meera Dewan* (Gift of Love, 1982) is a documentary about the dowry system, in which two dowry victims share their experiences. One had seventy per cent burns and died shortly after; the other was buried alive by her husband but miraculously survived (personal communication from Rinki Roy Bhattacharya). The situation of the Dalits is also being examined in film: such social issues have political implications. Chatterji's (1997) article is illuminating on the subject of political cinema in India. The problems with most documentaries are to do with marketing: where can they be shown and who will buy them?

In the Shadows

If the future of documentary film production looks promising, there is still one area in which conditions are far from satisfactory. Throughout the world, the glamour of the film industry – its stars in particular – is overwhelmingly emphasised. It is true that the rewards for those who make it big – stars, directors, producers, distributors and financiers – are enormous but for those who work behind the screen their existence is very often precarious and they have to live from hand to mouth. This is specially true of the Indian film industry which is not organised and relies on the whims and fancies of the movie moguls.

According to the *Report of the Working Group on National Film Policy* (1980), film production in 1978 represented an investment of Rs128 crores and in 1978-79 the net collections of the box office (excluding entertainment tax) were around Rs247 crores. Additionally, Rs13 crores were earned from the export of films (see Viegas, 1984). (This total of Rs260 crores is equivalent to about £47 million.) It was only after the filming of the controversial

TV documentary *Yeh Anjane*, portraying the harsh, naked exploitation which prevails in the world of junior artistes (as film extras are called) that a Casting Bureau was instituted. Nevertheless, according to Viegas, the promises and the dreams have not materialised. The film industry in India, as elsewhere, is riddled with favouritism and nepotism. In the early 1980s, the best junior artistes were paid Rs65 (i.e. about £1.15) for an eight hour shift and the job is casualised, so there are days when the artistes have no work at all. It is the Agents (also called suppliers) who decide who will be hand-picked for the shooting, presumably on a day to day basis. According to the artistes, only nationalisation can alleviate their plight.

CHAPTER 8

Regional Cinemas of India

Regional cinemas are the key to the Indian cinema industry. India is unique in its kaleidoscope of diverse languages and cultures: there are at least 15 languages and over 2000 dialects, and films are produced in most of the official languages. In 1993, for example, 183 films were made in Hindi, 168 in Tamil and 148 in Telugu. The largest number of films are produced in these three languages. However, 78 films were made in Kannada, 71 in Malayalam, 57 in Bengali, 35 in Marathi and almost 10 in Assamese.

This book's emphasis on the Bombay cinema is justifiable in that it represents Hindi-speaking films and is indeed synonymous with Indian popular cinema. Although we can talk of regional cinemas, there is an incessant cross-over of talents – Bengali film directors direct Hindi or Oriya films; Tamil directors direct Telugu films. Actors and actresses from the South play leading roles in films made in the North. Furthermore, some of the well-known figures in Indian cinema, particularly in the artistic tradition, come from the regional cinemas. The diverse regional cinemas in India strive to maintain their distinctive identities and provide an important dimension of the cultural wealth and diversity of India's regional cinemas.

One of the smallest film-producing regions, Assam, is in the extreme north east of India and its 20 million inhabitants speak Assamese and Bengali. The region is little known to the rest of India because of its remoteness. It is neglected; it depends heavily on agriculture and the only industries are tea and oil. According to Mazid (1996), such conditions were unfavourable to the birth of cinema, because filmmaking is an industrial activity.

Assam did not produce any silent films. Its first film, *Joymoti*, was produced in 1935 by Agarwalla, who drew on historical and literary sources to depict the tragic patriotism of a princess, while also portraying 'parallels with the situation of disorder and disharmony unleashed by the British rule on the people of Assam for aligning themselves with the National Movement' (Mazid, 1996:53). Although not a commercial success, it is notable that at a time when the Bombay cinema was producing mythological films, *Joymoti* was about an historical event.

A number of films (*Badan Barphukan*, 1948; *Lachit Barphukan*, 1960; *Maniram Dewan*, 1963) made from the 1940s to the 1960s were about personalities who sacrificed their lives for the cause of the Indian Freedom Movement. In 1964 Hazarika's *Pratidhwani* (The Echo) won him the President's Silver medal for the best film in Assamese. Based on a popular legend of the Khasi people, it 'tells the story of a poor shepherd boy and his love for a girl whom the hill King takes as his concubine. The film ends tragically with the shepherd boy being burnt alive' (Garga 1996:305).

The films produced since the 1970s include *Bristi* (Deluge, 1974), *Sandhyaraag* (Evening Song, 1977), *Sankalpat* (Line of Conviction, 1986), *Juge Juge Sangram* (Decades of Struggle, 1986) and *Sutrapat* (The Beginning, 1987). Most are about village life versus city life (*Sandhyaraag*) or about the Assam agitation which took place between 1979 and 1985. Both *Sankalpat* and *Juge Juge Sangram* are about justice for the Assamese people and the causes of the agitation.

Land disputes in rural Assam (*Halodhia Choraya Baodhan Khai*, The Catastrophe, 1978) and environmental concerns (*Banani*, Forest, 1989) are of considerable concern to the Assamese. Some of the films make only oblique references to the political issues. However, Gogoi's *Surya Tejor Anya Naam* (Sun is the Other Name of Blood) launched in 1991, is about the cause of independent Assam. Whether overt politics will become significant in Assamese cinema remains to be seen.

Jahnu Barua is one of Assam's best-known directors and has produced a number of remarkable films – *Aparoop* (1982), *Papoori* (1986), *Hkhagaroloi Boho Door* (It is a Long Way to the Sea, 1994). His *Haldhia Choraya Baodhan Khai* (already mentioned) won the Golden Lotus in India in 1988 and the Grand Prix for best film and best actor at Locarno (Garga 1996:307).

Kannada Cinema

Located in the state of Karnataka with over 40 million people and 1200 cinema halls (in 1993), Kannada cinema was to a large extent under the shadow of the neighbouring Tamil and Telugu film industries for a long time. Unlike Assamese cinema, the vast majority of the films produced in Kannada are of the popular variety – sentimental, melodramatic, escapist, full of songs and dance. However, a few filmmakers are keen to create a serious cinema that addresses significant social issues.

Mohan Bhavanami, the Chief Producer of the Film Division of the Government of India, made the first Kannada silent film, *Mricchakatika*, in 1929. In 1932 came two talkies, *Bhaktha Dhruva* and *Sati Sulochana*. At first the theatre provided the inspiration and artistic resources for the filmmakers, but cinema evolved somewhat sporadically until the 1950s. There were several reasons for this: the absence of entrepreneurship, lack of adequate technical facilities and the contentment of the audiences with seeing Hindi, Tamil and Telugu films. However, by the 1960s, the State Government decided to introduce subsidies for film production and to recognise good filmmaking by instituting an award system.

Samskara (Funeral Rites, 1970) by Telugu poet Pattabhi Rama Reddy has been discussed. A number of highly talented filmmakers followed Reddy: B.V. Karanth, Girish Karnad, G.V. Iyer and Girish Kasaravalli deserve special mention. Karanth's *Chomanadudi* (Chomana's Drum, 1975) highlights the strengths of the artistic cinema in Karnataka. Set in the 1930s, it concerns an old man, Chomana, who is filled with rage and despair over the poverty and social injustices he has daily to encounter. Only by playing his drum can he give expression to his pent-up feelings. He is perturbed by the humiliations that his children have to put up with. He dies an unhappy man, but the sound of his drum continues to arouse his fellow citizens.

Two years earlier, Girish Karnad made *Kaddu* (The Forest, 1973), set in the past and exploring the nature of violence that characterised feudal societies. Garga (1996: 281) remarked that 'The analysis of the socio-economic causes of feudal violence and decay is enriched by minutely observed details of village life and superstitions'.

We have also discussed films by directors Girish Kasaravelli and G. V. Iyer. Kasaravalli concerned himself with the 'stifling Brahminical orthodoxy that cloaks itself in puritanical ritual' and explores this theme in *Ghattashraddha* (The Ritual, 1977). Iyer's *Adi Shankaracharya* (1983), which won him the Golden Lotus, was the first feature film to be made in Sanskrit and is a tribute to the eighth century sage Shankara who, in the words of Garga (1996: 284), 'expounded the Advaita (non dualist) philosophy and who is to Hinduism what Saint Thomas Aquinas is to Christianity'.

Of the handful of women film directors in India who have gained national recognition, Prema Karanth is from Karnataka. We have discussed how her touching account of a child-widow, *Phaniyamma* (1982), so poignantly illustrates the problem of young widowhood (Garga 1996: 285). However, despite the outstanding success of such film directors, Kannada artistic cinema has yet to achieve its international repute or to produce filmmakers of the calibre of those working in Malayalam cinema.

Malayalam Cinema

The cinema of Kerala has achieved international recognition. This is due to the work of distinguished Malayalam film directors such as Adoor Gopalakrishnan, G. Aravindan and Shaji Karun. While popular films that bear the imprint of melodramatic musicals are produced in large numbers, the artistic cinema continues to grow. Kerala's literacy rates are the highest in India and there is a strong literary and theatre tradition that has aided this film culture.

We have already discussed Gopalakrishnan's *Elippathayam* (Rat Trap, 1981), which brought him international recognition and the British Film Institute Award as the 'maker of the most original and imaginative film' (Garga 1996: 271). His films such as *Chemmeen* (The Shrimp, 1968), *Mukhamukham* (Face to Face, 1984), *Ananthram* (Monologue, 1987) explore the concept of the self and the struggle to adapt to changing social circumstances.

The talent of the late G. Aravindan is evident in *Thampu* (The Circus Tent, 1978), *Kummaty* (The Bogeyman, 1979), *Esthappan* (Stephen, 1980) and *Pokkuveyil* (Twilight, 1981). *Thampu* explores the complex and lonely lives of circus-players 'with an almost documentary fidelity'. *Kummaty* deals with the legendary figure of a mysterious wizard who figures in children's lore in Kerala. Aravindan presents this character and children's reactions to him with poetic charm. *Esthappan* is set among Christian fishermen in Kerala and narrates the life of a wandering and mysterious spiritualist. *Pokkuveyil* is about a young poet who, unable to withstand the hard realities of life, slips into a world of fantasy and hallucination. The film has very little dialogue and relies on a rich use of colour. We have already discussed his *Chidambaram* (1985). This and his last film *Vasthuhara* (Dispossessed, 1990) confirm his sensitivity as a film maker.

In recent years, Shaji Karun, already distinguished as a cameraman, has emerged as a talented film director. His first feature film, *Piravi* (The Birth, 1988), was based on the Rajan murder case that occurred during the Emergency in the mid-1970s. It explores with great poetic sensitivity and cinematic understanding the anguished search of an old man for his lost son, who is reported to have been taken into police custody. *Piravi* won several prestigious awards at international film festivals and was shown in England on Channel 4.

While these filmmakers were making artistic films, the popular cinema in Kerala was catering to the escapist taste of the bulk of film goers, producing cheap entertainment. These films offer romance, sex, seduction and murder in abundance. As in many other states, the film industry in Kerala has had its ups and downs. At one point, money poured in from the Gulf states to shore up its film production but this is no longer the case. As with most popular cinema, the appeal of the films depends largely on the drawing power of the actors and actresses. In Kerala, actors such as Mammooty and Mohanlall, who have acted in hundreds of films, are eagerly sought by film producers. But Malayalam cinema deserves attention for its enriching of the artistic tradition of film.

Tamil Cinema

Unlike Malayalam cinema, Tamil cinema is not known for its serious and artistic films. It is characterised by its mawkishly sentimental films and its long link with politics. This connection between politics and cinema is perhaps the most noteworthy feature of the cinema of Tamil Nadu. We have already seen how such political figures as M.G. Ramchandran and Jayalalitha established their special identities through their work in cinema.

Chandralekha (1948), established the Tamil popular tradition of filmmaking and became a sensational success throughout India and beyond. Directed by S.S. Vasan, *Chandralekha* is a spectacular dance drama revolving around two royal brothers who fight for the throne and the hand of a beautiful maiden. It represents the clash of good and evil.

An important part of Tamil Nadu politics, as reflected, for example, in *Velaikkari* (1950), was to be anti-Brahmin and anti-establishment. The powerful and rhetorical dialogue focusing on social oppression made a strong impression on the people of Tamil Nadu, and the declamations made at the Mariamman Temple and the Court of Law appealed to the masses of people who were victims of diverse forms of social oppression.

However, there are very few films of artistic distinction and, despite the efforts of serious filmmakers like Balu Mahendra and K. Balachander, Tamil cinema continues to be known for its sentimental melodramas and its close alliance with politics. Mani Rathnam has recently emerged as a strong voice in Tamil filmmaking, combining popular appeal and technical sophistication in his work, as we saw in two of his most important films, *Roja* (1992) and *Bombay* (1994).

Telugu Cinema

Telugu cinema, too, has little to offer by way of serious and artistic work, although Hyderabad (Telugu) is one of the three most important film centres in India in terms of the number of films produced. The vast majority of Telugu films – mythological films as well as social dramas – are trite, highly melodramatic, often stagey, and are not known for the exploration of complex human experiences.

For many years N.T. Rama Rao, former Chief Minister of Andhra Pradesh, dominated the Telugu screen. He acted in over three hundred films and was well known for his portrayal of religious figures. In recent years, one or two determined filmmakers such as Narasinga Rao, have sought to introduce a serious note to Telugu cinema. In his first film *Rangula Kala* (A Colourful Dream, 1983), he plays the lead. The film portrays the tormented sensibility of a highly gifted modern painter, Ravi, and his growing social awareness and political consciousness. His film, *Dasi* (Bonded Woman, 1988) won five national awards and gained him national recognition as a distinguished film-maker in India. *Dasi* deals with the way in which young girls from poor peasant families were bought by rich families as bonded labour. But despite the best efforts of artists like Narasinga Rao, Telugu cinema, with its large annual film output, has yet to develop a sophisticated film culture.

Marathi Cinema

Many film historians would designate Maharashtra as the birthplace of Indian cinema. The name of D.G. Phalke is honoured as the father of Indian cinema. Early on, there were a number of Marathi film directors who showed talent and commitment to the growth of Indian film culture. V. Shantaram, Damle, Fatehlal, Master Vinayak and also P.L. Deshpande, G.D. Madgulkar, Raja Paranjpe and Sudhir Phadke are perhaps most significant. However, as an art form and industry it has had its share of problems: Most films made in Marathi are cheap and commercial, often modelled on Hindi films, and they cater to the escapist desires of the majority of film-goers. In terms of experience, style and technique, there is little to recommend them. However, despite this commercial film culture, a number of directors have recently sought to create a vibrant artistic cinema in Maharashtra, among them Jabhar Patel, Amol Palekar, Nachiket and Jayoo Patwardhan and Vijaya Metha.

Jabbar Patel, a physician by profession, has been closely involved with the theatre. His first film. *Samna* (The Confrontation, 1975), based on a script by Vijay Tendulkar, dramatises the conflict of wills between a small-town political racketeer and a morally upright school teacher. His next film, *Jait Re Jait* (The Victory, 1977) tells the story of a tribal youth, 'the son of a

Samna village oracle, who loses faith in his god when his father dies of a snake bite and his fiancée is stung to death by the poisonous bees from the holy mountain' (Garga, 1996: 293). But the film that perhaps established most strongly Jabbar Patel's reputation for serious moral concern was *Umbartha* (The Threshold, 1981). The film centres on the life of Sulabha, a young woman who has a diploma in social work and is married into an upper middle class family. Her mother-in-law, herself a social worker, would like Sulabha to join her in her work. But Sulabha accepts a position at an office some three hundred miles from her home. She has a husband and a five year old daughter, but she is equally attracted to her job and the film charts the way that she negotiates these conflicting loyalties.

Nachitet and Jayoo Patwardhan's *22 June 1897* (1979) cinematises a violent episode in Indian history. Damodar Chapekar, the eldest of three sons of a preacher singer, leads a group of militant Brahmin youths who are determined to challenge two of the elements of British imperialism – the English language and Christianity. Damodar plans to kill Walter Rand, a British officer and the film deals with this incident and its aftermath.

Like Prema Karanth in Karnataka, Vijaya Metha is one of the few distinguished women film directors in India. Her film *Smriti Chitre* (Episodes from Memory, 1983) won the National Award for the best Marathi language film of that year and constitutes a probing examination of the Brahmin tradition as a cultural force. The film is set in the early twentieth century and deals with the lives of Narayan Vanan Tilak and his wife, Laxmibai. In accordance with custom, they are married while they are still children. At her husband's request, she educates herself. Surprisingly, her husband, a Brahmin scholar, decides to become a Christian. She is caught between the loyalty to her husband and loyalty to the religious tradition in which she was brought up.

Amol Palekar acted in Basu Chatterji's *Rajnigandha* (1994) and his first film *Akriet* (The Misbegotten, 1981) won many awards at international film festivals. The film is based on a series of violent murders among tribals in Maharashtra. In 1990, he produced *Thodasa Rumani Ho Jaye* (Let's Get Romantic), a mass-entertainment musical. These, then, are among a handful of Marathi filmmakers who are seeking to improve the quality of Marathi filmmaking. Many of them have also directed Hindi films.

Bengali Cinema

Of all the regional cinemas it is Bengal that won for Indian cinema widespread international acclaim. We have already considered three of the most important and famous Bengali film directors: Satyajit Ray, Ritwik Ghatak and Mrinal Sen. Of the young and promising filmmakers, we have also discussed Goutam Ghosh's *Antarjali Yatra* (The Voyage Beyond, 1987) and Aparna Sen's *36 Chowringhee Lane* (1981).

Most critics, when writing about regional cinemas in India, will focus on Bengali cinema. A rich film culture continues to characterise Bengali cinema and the very active film society movement played a significant role in shaping the peoples's taste and widening their cinematic horizons. The interaction between the literary culture and film culture was also beneficial. Mahatma Gandhi is reported to have said that what Bengal thinks today, the rest of India thinks tomorrow. In much the same way, Bengali cinema has led in subject matter from the 1920s till the middle of the 1940s. And the way Rabindranath Tagore's work has been creatively used by Satyajit Ray and others enhances the film culture. Garga (1996: 307) rightly asserts that:

In a situation where much of Indian cinema is homogenised and moribund, the regional film has given it an identity and a sense of purpose. It has also revealed the variety of peoples and cultures in India with their richly diverse languages, legends, stories, clothes, climate, music and dance.

Talking of music and dance reminds us that missing from our discussion of India's regional cinemas is Punjabi cinema, which has suffered substantially since partition and deserves support and encouragement.

CHAPTER 9
Conclusion

This book has reviewed the almost century-old Indian Cinema. What will be its future shape and direction? At a seminar on the future of the Indian cinema organised at the Nehru Centre in London in 1997, some film critics – particularly two from Britain – were pessimistic about the new trends and future shape of Indian cinema, both artistic and popular.

There is no doubt that many of the newest films – for instance, *Hero No.1, Daava, Gupt* – explain their pessimism. For, in addition to the themes of violence, vengeance and rape which characterise the Indian cinema of the 1980s and 1990s, there is now a pattern of dance sequences which is rather callisthenic and repetitive – Govinda and Karisma Kapoor, Sanjay Dutt and Madhuri Dixit, Shah Ruk Khan and Kajol are all at it. The redeeming features of some of these films are the usual, time-honoured, beautifully evocative music and songs. At one level, Indian popular cinema, since its beginnings but particularly in the 1940s, 1950s and 1960s, has helped communal relations. With the exception of the Hindu mythological dramas, it has been secularist and pluralist. At another level, its superficiality, vulgarity and crudeness (in the worst examples) have provided a uni-dimensional and chauvinistic image of Hindi-speaking North India. This, according to Das Gupta (1991:268-269), is due mainly to the Bombay producers who, in targeting a lumpen audience, pitch their films at the 'lowest-common-denominator consumer'.

> Smuggling, profiteering and other components of the substructures of traditional mercantilism have increasingly constituted the Hindi cinema's lifeline since Independence ... The film financier is not the MBA from Harvard or its Indian counterpart, he has descended from the 'bania' (mercantile) tradition and remains firmly wedded to it, far removed from the industrial entrepreneur of the post-colonial period ...'

are some of Das Gupta's (1991) criticisms. Artists have complained that money is the sole criterion of the industry today. Sunil Dutt (father of Sanjay) said recently: 'I cannot understand this industry where dedication and discipline mean nothing, where money is the only thing that matters' (*Screen*, 1997:20). Rishi Kapoor has been quoted as saying: 'If the 1950s and 1960s were the golden age of Indian cinema, today it's the cardboard age of Indian cinema. The more thin and flimsy, the better perhaps'. (*Filmfare*, 1997:93)

However, while a significant number of Indian films are likely to be box-office failures, a few – very few – will endear themselves to the audience. They will rise above the customary mediocrity and music, song and dance will continue to enhance their success. *Border*, for example, has become hugely popular aided by its ten-minute song *Sandeshi Aate Hain*, which is used to advertise the film.

As far as the future shape and direction of the Indian cinema is concerned, much will depend on how India faces the new millennium. And there are already indications that politically, socially and economically the India of the next century will be very different. We have shown that Indian cinema is shaped by the country's political, social and economic conditions. And these are changing.

Politically, the long period of single party rule at national level is over. India is being increasingly governed by coalitions – a trend that is likely to continue, in at least the early decades of the next century. The decline of the Nehru-Gandhi dynasty and the rise of the parties of Hindu nationalist orientation – the Bharatiya Janata Party (BJP) is now the second largest party – are restructuring the political dynamics of India. Experience suggests that coalition governments imply some instability.

Economically, however, the picture is much brighter. It has been predicted that by the year 2020, 'India is expected to be the fourth largest economy in the world in terms of purchasing power parity, after China, the United States and Japan' (Gupta, 1997:305). According to Gupta, India has to some degree already caught up with the first stage of the post-industrial revolution 'in the form of personal computers, fax machines, e-mail and cellular phones': Multinationals such as IBM, Texas Instruments, Motorola have already installed themselves in India and, although the pace of change has so far been moderate, 'its seven per cent economic growth and its change of direction towards the East in terms of new trading patterns, are likely to propel India much more rapidly into the league of economic giants of the ASEAN countries'.

The social consequences are likely to be revolutionary. Although the Nehru-Gandhi dynasty provided a period of political stability (except in the last years of Mrs Gandhi's rule), two of its major issues, Untouchability and poverty, have yet to be resolved. Gupta (1997) has described a spectacular empowerment in recent years of the intermediate castes (also known as Other Backward Classes or OBCs) by allocating them 30 per cent reserved representation in all services except the armed forces. And the recent appointment of Kocheril Raman Narayan, an 'untouchable', to the office of President of India – the highest office in the land – is an indication that caste is no longer the prison that it was.

Poverty, however, is a more intractable issue. In a recent study, Kakar (1996) argues that the Indian way of thinking changes only slowly and Indian culture is basically change-resistant. Consequently, the great masses of the illiterate and poor will take some time to come out of their poverty. As long as the social and cultural make-up of the Indian population remains static, Indian popular cinema as it is now will continue to appeal. From its beginnings, cinema halls have been one of the few venues of entertainment open to all regardless of their race, class, religion or caste. The themes and stories may change and the influence of multimedia, satellite and cable might well lessen the impact on the audience of Indian popular films.

Politics has become more transparent and disadvantaged groups in India have become more organised and more vocal. The artistic cinema has always explored social issues and sought to expose injustice and as long as funding for artistic films continues, so, too, will serious films.

More difficult to predict is the influence in the new millennium of films made by Asians in the diaspora. We have seen how in Canada and in Britain, serious contributions to the artistic genre are emerging. Some offer fresh perspectives, particularly feminist ones; some explore new experiences, notably of living as immigrants in the West. Considering the large diaspora audience potential, this may well generate a significant body of work for the large screen as well as the small.

We have made clear that this book is intended primarily for the general reader with little knowledge of Indian cinema, as well as for the better informed. Our audience is primarily British, although we hope students and readers from elsewhere will also find it useful. We have not sought to discuss or even list all the significant films made in India during the past nine decades, but rather, have chosen to focus on some representative examples that delineate the broad contours of Indian cinema. There are bound to be omissions of films and filmmakers in a broad survey of the terrain for non-specialist readers.

Although our focus of interest has been on popular cinema, this is best understood in relation to artistic cinema. So along with popular cinema we have discussed artistic cinema in India, as a way of pointing out the significant differences and occasional affinities of interest.

Throughout the book, we have sought to situate Indian films in their cultural context. Films open up a window onto the wider cultural world. By watching Indian films, and by exploring them sensitively, we can attain a deeper understanding of Indian culture and of its history, politics and values. This approach has allowed us to point out the distinctiveness of Indian cinema more clearly and contextualise contemporary films more productively.

In the final analysis, what is most important is that we begin to see and appreciate Indian films with enhanced critical understanding. This book has been written with that hope in mind. By seeing more and more Indian films not only will we understand Indian society and culture better but also, through comparisons and contrasts, the society and culture in which we live.

Appendix

NFDC Bombay
Number of films sold and revenue from key export markets for Indian films, 1988

Country	No. of films	Revenue (Rs)
Arabian Gulf	179	24,349,000
USSR	18	9,811,000
Indonesia	41	9,484,000
Sri Lanka	30	2,588,000
Burma .	17	2,463,00
UK & Ireland	67	2,286,000
Morocco	36	2,031,000
Jordan	28	1,814,000
Fiji Islands	29	1,785,000
Singapore	27	1,642,000
Mauritius	61	1,632,000
Sudan	31	1,288,000
Tanzania	28	1,281,000
Maldives	27	1,214,000
Kenya	22	1,086,000
Malaysia	33	808,000
Yemen, Djibouti, Sanna	13	761,000
West Indies	13	590,000
South/Latin America	12	524,000
Gambia	11	536,000
Nigeria	10	451,000
Liberia	10	331,000

Source: *NFDC, Bombay. From the Asian Film Industry* by John A. Lent (1990) London: C. Helm.

References and Further Reading

ARMES, R. (1987) *Third World Film Making and the West* Berkeley: University of California Press

ARNOLD, A. (1988) 'Popular Film Song In India: A Case of Mass Market Musical Eclecticism' in *Popular Music* Vol.7 No.2 May pp.177-188

ARNOLD, A. (1991) 'Hindi Film Git' Doctoral Dissertation submitted to the University of Illinois at Urbana-Champaign

ARNOLD, D. and HARDIMAN, D. (Eds) (1994) 'Subaltern Studies' Vol. VIII Delhi: Oxford University Press

ARORA, P. (1995) 'Imperilling the Prestige of the White Woman Colonial Anxiety' in *Visual Anthropology Review and Film Censorship in British India* Vol.II No.2 Fall pp. 36-50

BAILY, J. (1995) 'The Role of Music in Three Bristish Muslim Communities' in *Diaspora* Vol.1 No.4 pp. 77-88

BANERJI, S. (1988) 'Ghazals to Bhangra in Great Britain' in *Popular Music* Vol.7 No.2 pp. 207-214

BARNOUW, E. and KRISHNASWAMY, S. (1963) *Indian Film* New York: Columbia University Press

BASU, S, KAK, S. and KRISHEN, P. (1980) 'Cinema and Society: A Search for Meaning in a New Genre' in KRISHEN, P. (Ed) *India International Centre Quarterly* Vol.8, No.1, March pp. 57-76

BEEMAN, W.O. (1980) 'The use of Music in Popular Film: East and West' in KRISHEN, P. (Ed) *India International Centre Quarterly* Vol.8, No.1, March pp. 77-88

BHARUCHA, R. (1995) *Chandralekha Woman Dance Resistance* New Delhi: Harper Collins

BHATTACHARYA, R. (1990) 'Breaking Mind Blocks about Documentaries' in *Montreal Serai* April/May

BHATTACHARYA, G. and GABRIEL, J. (1994) 'Gurinder Chadha and the Apna Generation' in *Third Text* No1.27 Summer pp. 55-63

BHOWMICK, S. (1995) 'Film Censorship' in Maitra P. (Ed) *100 years of Cinema*, Calcutta: Nandan

BINFORD, M.R. (1989) 'Indian Popular Cinema' in *Quarterly Review of Film and Video* Vol.II, pp.1-9

BROWN, J. (1994) *Modern India* Second Edition, Oxford: Oxford University Press

BRUCE, S. (1995) *Religion in Modern Britain* Oxford University Press

CHAKRAVARTY, S.S. (1989) 'National Identity and the Realist Aesthetic: Indian Cinema of the Fifties' in *Quarterly Review of Film and Video* Vol.11, pp.31-48

CHAKRAVARTY, S.S. (1996) *National Identity in Indian Popular Cinema* (1947-1987) Delhi: Oxford University Press

CHANDRA, M. (1973) *The World of Courtesans* Delhi: Oxford University Press

CHANDRA, M. (1994) 'Music Mania' in *India Today* November 15.

CHATTERJEE, G. (1992) *Awara* New Delhi: Wiley Eastern Ltd

CHATTERJEE, P. (1993) *The Nation and its Fragments* Princeton: Princeton University Press

CHATTERJEE, P. (1994) 'The Indian Documentary Scene Fraught with Hazards' in *Cinemaya* No.23 pp. 44-45

CHATTERJEE, P. (1995) 'A Bit of Song and Dance' in VASUDEV, A. (Ed) *Frames of Mind* New Delhi: UBPSD

CHATTERJI, S. A. (1997) 'The Politics of Parallel Cinema' in *Deep Focus* Vol.VII No.1 pp. 74-82

DANDA, D. (1997) 'Bandit Queen – A Semiotic Approach' in *Deep Focus* Vol.II No.2 pp 34-40

DAS GUPTA, C. (1991) *The Painted Face: Studies in India's Popular Cinema* New Delhi: Roli Books

DAS, V. (1988) 'Shakti Versus Sati – A Reading of the Santoshi Ma Cult' in *Manushi* No.49, pp. 26-30

DHARAP. B. V. (1973) *Indian Films Pune*: Motion Picture Enterprise

DHILLON-KASHYAP, D. (1988) 'Locating the Asian Experience' in *Screen* Vol.29, No.4, Autumn pp. 120-126

DHONDY, F. (1985) 'Keeping Faith: Indian Film and its World' in *Daedalus* Fall, pp. 125-140

DISSAYANAKE W. (Ed) (1988) *Cinema and Cultural Identity: Reflection on Films from Japan, Indian and China* Lanham: University Press of America

DISSAYANAKE W. and SAHAI, M. (1992) *Sholay: A Cultural Reading* Honolulu: Wiley: East West

DISSAYANAKE W. (1993) (Ed) *Melodrama and Asian Cinema* Cambridge: Cambridge University Press

DORAISWAMY, R. (1994) 'Changing Narrative Strategies' in *Cinemaya* No.23 pp. 4-12

DUTT, S. (1997) 'A Great Indian, a Great Man' in *Screen* 20 June

GARGA, B. D, (1996) *So Many Cinemas* Mumba: Eminence Designs

GEETHA, J. (1990) 'The Mutating Mother' in *Deep Focus* Vol.III,1 No.3 pp.9-15

GHOSH, B. (1992) 'Satyajit Raj's Devi: Constructing a Third World Feminist – Critique' in *Screen* Vol.33 No.2 Summer pp.165-173

GOPALAN, L. (1997) Avenging Women in Indian Cinema' in *Screen* Vol.38, No.1, pp. 42-59

GOPINATH, G. (1995) 'Bombay, U.K. Yuba City' Bhangra Music and the Engendering of Diaspora in *Diaspora* Vol.4 No.3 pp. 303-321

GUPTA, B. S. (1997) 'India in the Twenty-First Century' in *International Affairs* Vol.73 No.2 pp. 297-314

HOUSDEN, R. (1996) *Travels Through Sacred India* New Delhi: Harper Collins

HARDGRAVE, Jr R. L. (1975) *When Stars Displace the Gods: The Folk Culture of Cinema in Tamil Nadu* in Occasional Paper Series No.2 Centre for Asian Studies – University of Texas, pp. 1-23

IMAX, (1996) *A Bigger Vision – Celebrating 100 Years of Cinema* London: British Film Institute

JAIN, R. D. (1960) *The Economic Aspects of the Film Industry in India* Delhi: Atma Ram and Sons

JOSEPH, A. and SHARMA, K. (Ed) (1994) *Whose News? The Media and Women's Issues* New Delhi: Sage

KABIR, M. N. (1991) *Indian Film Music* Postgraduate Seminar Aspects of Commonwealth Literature – Institute of Commonwealth Studies, University of London, 21 October

KABIR, M. N. and SNELL, R. (1994) 'Bollywood Nights: The Voices Behind the Stars of Indian Film Music' in BROUGHTON, S., ELLINGHAM, M., MUDDYMAN, D. and TRILLO, R. (Eds) *World Music – The Rough Guide* London: Rough Guides Ltd.

KAKAR, S. (1996) *The Indian Psyque* Delhi: Oxford University Press

KAPOOR, R. (1997) 'Quote ... Unquote' in *Filmfare* June

KAVIRAJ, S. (1994) 'Crisis of the Nation-State in India' in *Political Studies XLII*, pp. 115-129

KAZMI, N. (1996) *Ire in the Soul – Bollywood's Angry Years* New Delhi: Harper Collins

KHANNA, S. (1980) 'Indian Cinema and Indian Life Vol.III of Hindi-Urdu Films for instructional purposes. Centers for South and Southeast Asia Studies, Berkeley: University of California

KOHLI, A. (1990) *Democracy and Discontent: India's Growing Crisis of Governability* Cambridge: Cambridge University Press

KOTHARI, R. (1988) *State Against Democracy* New Delhi: Ajanta Publication

KRISHEN, P. (1980) 'Indian Popular Cinema Myth, Meaning and Metaphor' *Indian International Centre* Quarterly Special Issue, Vol.8, No.1, March

LEVICH, J. (1997) 'The undiscovered Art of Ritwik Ghatak' in *Film Comment* Vol.33 No.2 March/April pp. 30-35

MADAN, T. N. (1989) 'Religion in India' in *Proceedings of the American Academy of Arts and Sciences* Vol.118, No.4, pp. 115-146

MAITRA, P. (Ed) (1995) *100 Years of Cinema* Calcutta:Nandan.

MAJUMDAR, D. (1995) Indian Film Industry in MAITRA, P. (Ed) *100 years of Cinema* Calcutta: Nandan

MANUEL, P. (1988) 'Popular Music in India 1901-1986' in *Popular Music* Vol.7 No.2 May pp. 157-176

MANUEL, P. (1993) *Cassette Culture: Popular Music and Technology in North India* Chicago: University of Chicago Press

MAZID, A.. (1996) 'Sixty Years of Cinema from Arsam. Close Up of the Socio-political Image' in *Deep Focus* Vol.VI Nos.2 & 3 pp. 52-59

MISHRA, V. (1985) 'Towards a Theoretical Critique of Indian Cinema' in *Screen* May-August Vol.26, Nos.3-4

MISHRA, V., JEFFREY, P. and SHOESMITH, B. (1989) 'The Actor as Parallel Text in Bombay Cinema' in *Quarterly Review of Film and Video* Vol.11, pp.49-67

MITAL, A. (1995) *Cinema Industry in India – Pricing and Taxation* New Delhi: Indus Publishing Co

MITRA, A. (1994) 'An Indian Religious Soap Opera and the Hindu Image' in *Media, Culture and Society* Vol.16 pp. 149-155

MUKHOPADHYAY, D. (1995) *The Maverick Maestro – Mrinal Sen* New Delhi: Harper Collins

MULVEY, L (1975) 'Visual Pleasure and Narrative Cinema' in *Screen* Vol.16, No.3 (Atumn) pp.6-18

MULVEY, L. (1989) *Visual and Other Pleasures*, Bloomington: Indiana University Press

NANDY, A. (1981) 'The Popular Hindi Film Ideology and First Principles in India' *India International Centre* Quarterly Special Issue, Vol.8, No.1, March pp. 89-96

NANDY, A. (1987-88) 'An Intelligent Critic's Guide to Indian Cinema' Part I, II and III, December 1987, June 1988

NANDY, A. (1997) *The Secret Politics of Our Desires* Zed Books forthcoming

NEGI, M. (1994-5) 'Mira Nair' in *Cinemaya* Autumn/Winter pp. 25-27

NELMES, J. (Ed) (1996) *An introduction to Film Studies* London: Routledge

NEWCOMB, H. (1997) *Encyclopaedia of Television Volumes I, II and III*, Fitzroy: Dearborn

NIRANJANA, T. 'Integrating whose Nation? Tourists and Terrorists in Roja' in *Economic and Political Weekly* January 15, pp.79-82

OOMEN, M. A. and JOSEPH, K. V. (1991) *Economics of Indian Cinema* New Delhi: Oxford and IBH Publishing Co

OOMEN, T. K. (1990) *State and Society in India: Studies in Nation Building* New Delhi: Sage Publication

PARANJPYE, S. (1988) 'Women in Cinema' in *Cinema in India* Vol.11 No.1 Jan-April pp. 15-19

PENDAKUR, M. (1989) 'New Cultural Technologies and the Fading Glitter of Indian Cinema' in *Quarterly Review of Film and Video*, Vol.11 pp. 69-78

PENDAKUR, M. (1995) 'Cinema of Resistance: – Recent Trends in Indian Documentary Film' Paper presented at the Yamagata International Documentary Film Festival, Tokyo, September pp.1-4

PENDAKUR, M. (1996) 'India's National Film Policy' in Moran, A. (Ed) *Film Policy* London: Routledge

PENDAKUR, M. and SUBRAMANYAM, R. (1996) 'Indian Cinema Beyond National Borders' in SINCLAIR, J. (Ed) *New Patterns in Global Television: Peripheral Vision* Oxford: Oxford University Press

PRICE, S. (1994) *Media Studies* London: Pitman

PRASAD, M. M. (1994) 'The State and Culture: Hindi Cinema on the Passive Revolution' Doctoral Dissertation submitted to the University of Pittsburgh

RAINA, M. Z. (1986) ''I'm All Right Jack': Packaged Pleasures of the Middle Cinema' in *Journal of Popular Culture* Vol.20 Fall pp. 131-141

RAJADHYAKSHA, A. and WILLEMEN, P. (1994) *Encyclopaedia of Indian Cinema* New Delhi: Oxford University Press

RAMCHANDRAN, T. M. (Ed) (1985) *70 Years of Indian Cinema (1913-1983)* Bombay: Cinema India-International

RAO, L. (1989) 'Woman in Indian Films – A Paradigm of Continuity and Change' in *Media, Culture and Society* Vol.11 pp. 443-458

RAO, M. (1988) 'Victims in Vigilante Clothing' in *Cinema in India* Oct.-Dec. pp.24-26

RAO, M. (1995) 'To be a Woman....' in VASUDEV, A. (Ed) *Frames of Mind* New Delhi: UBSPD

RAY, M. and JACKA, E. (1996) 'Indian Television: An Emerging Regional Force' in SINCLAIR, J. (Ed) *New Patterns in Global Television: Peripheral Vision* Oxford: Oxford University Press

RICHARDS, A. (1995) *Hidden Pleasures: Negotiating the Myth of the Female Ideal in Popular Hindi Cinema* (Paper circulated at the SOAS Conference) 19-21 June

SARKAR, B. (1995) 'Epic (Mis)takes: Nation, Religion and Gender on Television' in *Quarterly Review of Film and Video* Vol.16 No.1 pp. 59-75

SEN, A. (1993) 'Indian Pluralism' in *Monsoon* Vol.20, No.3, pp. 27-46

SHARMA, S. D. (1994) 'India's precarious democracy: Between Crisis and resilience' review article in *Contemporary South Asia* Vol.3 No.2 pp.145-163

SHRIDAR, K. T. (1989) 'An Elegy to Bombay' in *Deep Focus* Vol.2 No.1 September pp. 55-56

SINGH, S. (1989) 'The Epic (on) Tube: Plumbing the Depths of History' in *Cinema in India* Vol.3 No.2 pp. 77-101

SPIVAK, GAYATRI CHAKRAVORTY (1988) 'Can the Subaltern Speak?' in NELSON, C. AND GROSSBERG L. (Eds) *Marxism and the Interpretation of Culture* Urbane: University of Illinois Press

SUBRAMANYAN, R. (1996) 'Class, Caste and Performance in 'Subaltern' Feminist Film Theory and Praxis: An Analysis of Rudaali' in *Cinema Journal* Vol.35, No.3 Spring pp. 34-57

THOMAS, R. (1985) Indian Cinema: Pleasures and Popularity in *Screen* Vol.26 No.3-4 pp. 116-131

THOMAS, R. (1987) 'Mythologies and Modern India' in LUHR, W. (Ed) *World Cinema Since 1945* New York: Ungar

THOMAS, R. (1989) 'Sanctity and Scandal – the Mythologisation of Mother India' in *Quarterly Review of Film and Video* Vol.11, No.3 Winter pp.11-30

THOMAS, R. (1995) *Mother India Maligned: Film and Politics in Modern India – The Saga of Sanjay Dutt* (Paper circulated at the SOAS Conference) 19-21 June

UBEROI, P. (1995) *Imagining the Family: An Ethnography of Viewing 'Hum Aapke Hain Koun..!* Paper presented at the SOAS Conference on 'The Consumption of Popular Culture in India', 19-21 June

VALICHA, K. (1988) *The Moving Image* Hyderabad: Orient Longman Limited

VARSHNEY, A.. (1993) 'Contested Meanings: India's National Identity, Hindu Nationalism and the Politics of Anxiety' in *Daedalus* Vol.122, No.3, pp 227-261.

VASUDEV, A. (1986) *The New Indian Cinema* Delhi: Macmillan.

VASUDEV, A. (1995) *Frames of Mind Reflections on Indian Cinema* New Delhi: UBSPD.

VASUDEVAN, R. S. (1989) 'The Melodramatic Mode and the Commercial Hindi Cinema: Notes on Film History, Narrative and Performance in the 1950s' in *Screen* Vol.30 No.3.

VASUDEVAN, R. S. (1991) The Cultural Space of a Film Narrative: Interpreting Kismet (Bombay Talkies, 1943) in *The Indian Economic and Social History Review* Vol.28 No.2 pp. 171-185

VASUDEVAN, R. S. (1995a) 'Film Studies, New Cultural History and Experience of Modernity' in *Economic and Political Weekly* November 4 pp.2809-2814

VASUDEVAN, R. S. (1995b) *Bombay and its Public* (Paper circulated at the SOAS Conference) 19-21 June

VIEGAS, S. (1984) 'Lost in the Shadows' in *The Illustrated Weekly of India* February 12, pp. 40-45

WADIA, R. V. (1993) *Fearless: The Hunterwali Story* (75 minutes documentary).

INDEX

Films referred to in this bok are in italics. For a full filmography of India see *Encyclopaedia of Indian Cinema* (1994).

—C—

—D—

—E—